"A wonderfully readable synthesis of attachment theory, mindfulness, and cutting-edge approaches to developing self-awareness. This is illustrated throughout with practical advice and vivid stories told by a wise and caring therapist, who is a recognized expert on cultivating successful relationships."

—**Diane Handlin, PhD**, founder and executive director of the Mindfulness-Based Stress Reduction Center, NJ

"Leslie Becker-Phelps explains how early attachments can create obstacles to healthy and secure connections in adult romantic relationships. *Insecure in Love* provides the self-knowledge and the tools necessary to overcome these obstacles and get you closer to feeling secure, happy, and loved in your relationships. Highly recommended for anyone who feels anxious and insecure in a relationship."

—**Michelle Skeen, PsyD**, author of *The Critical Partner* and host of *Relationships 2.0* on KCAA 1050-AM

"You are worthy of love, genuine happiness, and intimacy—and *Insecure in Love* will help you to finally know it. Encouraging, understanding, and supportive every step of the way, Leslie Becker-Phelps guides you through a transformational journey of self-discovery as you break through your barriers to love and experience true change and healing.

"If you're single, you'll discover how to choose a partner who is truly available for a connected, supportive, nurturing relationship—someone who accepts and loves you for you. If you're in a relationship, you will gain insight into your partner's behavior and motivation and discover how to create a loving connection in which you both feel truly valued and cared for.

"Filled with relevant, real-life examples and powerful exercises, *Insecure in Love* will help you leave your self-criticism and sabotaging behaviors behind and develop true self-compassion. No matter how much you've struggled in the past, you will finally understand how to create happy, healthy relationships and experience true, lasting love."

—**Mali Apple** and **Joe Dunn**, authors of *The Soulmate Experience: A Practical Guide to Creating Extraordinary Relationships*

"It is rare that an author can take such a deep and meaningful subject and present it in a helpful, caring, and hopeful manner. Those who are suffering from anxiety disorders that have undermined past relationships will find her suggestions and exercises easy to understand and potentially very successful."

—**Randi Gunther, PhD**, author of *Relationship Saboteurs*

"Motivated by her professional interest in humans and attachment theory, Dr. Becker-Phelps has developed a solid resource for men and women to improve their lives and their relationships. *Insecure in Love* is a clear and comprehensive guide for self-understanding and self-compassion in which readers are encouraged to explore themselves and complete step-by-step exercises. The end result will be greater understanding of your relationships and a healthier, more secure self!"

—**Kathryn Cortese, MSW, LCSW, ACSW**, co-owner and president of *Gürze-Salucore Eating Disorders Resource Catalogue*

"*Insecure in Love* is engaging, practical, and comprehensive all at the same time. It takes the latest theories of love and provides a useful roadmap for why couples struggle to maintain closeness. Becker-Phelps gets to the heart of the challenge and describes what individuals need to address about themselves, as well as what couples can work on together, in order to recreate a meaningful connection between two people."

—**Daniel Goldberg, PhD**, director at the New Jersey Couples Training Program in the Center for Psychotherapy and Psychoanalysis of New Jersey

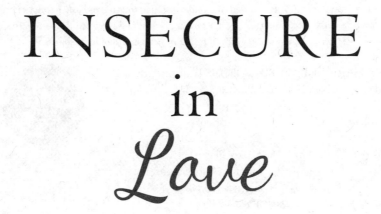

INSECURE
in
Love

How
ANXIOUS ATTACHMENT
Can Make You Feel Jealous,
Needy, *and* Worried *and*
What You Can Do About It

LESLIE BECKER-PHELPS, PhD

New Harbinger Publications, Inc.

NEW HARBINGER PUBLICATIONS is a registered trademark of New Harbinger Publications, Inc.

Distributed in Canada by Raincoast Books

Copyright © 2014 by Leslie Becker-Phelps
New Harbinger Publications, Inc.
5674 Shattuck Avenue
Oakland, CA 94609
www.newharbinger.com

All Rights Reserved

Acquired by Melissa Kirk; Cover design by Amy Shoup;
Edited by Ken Knabb; Text design by Tracy Marie Carlson

Library of Congress Cataloging-in-Publication Data

Becker-Phelps, Leslie.
  Insecure in love : how anxious attachment can make you feel jealous, needy, and worried and what you can do about it / Leslie Becker-Phelps.
     pages cm
  Includes bibliographical references.
  ISBN 978-1-60882-815-9 (paperback) -- ISBN 978-1-60882-816-6 (pdf e-book) -- ISBN 978-1-60882-817-3 (epub) 1. Love. 2. Man-woman relationships. 3. Self-consciousness (Awareness) 4. Anxiety. I. Title.
  BF575.L8.B33 2014
  152.4'1--dc23

                              2014011349

Printed in the United States of America

24   23   22

25   24   23   22   21   20

Contents

PART FOUR
Lighting Up Your Love Life

Acknowledgments

There are innumerable people to thank for helping shape the ideas I've laid out in this book. At the top of this list are those whom I've treated in therapy. My experience with them has very directly shaped the psychologist I am and the one I am becoming. I thank them all for opening their lives and hearts to me.

Then there are those who have more directly contributed to this book. My husband, Mark Phelps, has been a loving support, a cheerleader, and an expert editor. As a professional journalist, he is perpetually engrossed in writing articles; so from watching the two of us, our sons—Marcus and Elijah—have declared that they don't want to be writers when they grow up.

This book, of course, would not exist in its current form without the folks at New Harbinger Publications. I appreciate their confidence in me, a first-time author, and their guidance and encouragement through the whole process. The supportive, timely, and experienced feedback from Melissa Kirk and Jess Beebe was especially helpful.

I also owe much to friends and colleagues who have been supportive. Charles Mark, Kathy Cortese, and Jennifer Brown were particularly helpful in sharing their personal thoughts and professional expertise. I owe them more than I think even they realize. In addition, Steve Glass was kind enough to share his insights, as well as his excitement about meditation, both of which I greatly appreciate.

Introduction

And you lived happily ever after...

Or at least you would if only you could be more interesting or more attractive; or if you weren't so needy; or if you could figure out what's wrong with you that makes your relationships never work out well. Maybe you've been with a partner for a long time, but you struggle with feeling that your partner keeps falling short and will never fill that hole in your heart. You also suspect that *you* are part of the problem.

Whether single or in a relationship, many people believe that they'll never be happy in love. They feel lonely and want companionship—not just a buddy to sit next to at a movie, but a friend, confidante, and lover to accompany them through that greatest of all adventures we call life. They often fear that their partners will bolt once they get to know "the real me." Sometimes they feel that their partners appreciate the things they do. But this isn't enough. After all, what if their performance falters? Then there's the ever-present concern of whether anyone would truly be there for them if they let themselves be vulnerable by looking to that person for support, comfort, and reassurance.

If you relate to any of these struggles, then this book is for you.

As a clinical psychologist, I have treated many people with diverse variations on these themes. Over the years, they have opened their hearts and their lives to me, hoping for positive change—and I believe that most of them found it. Therapy provided them a way to discover the love they sought. It helped them to find inner healing and to choose partners who offered genuine love. With wiser choices, they created opportunities for growth and further healing. The result was that they improved their ability to enjoy and nurture happier, healthier relationships.

You, like many of my patients, may be armed with lots of information, expert advice, or a "proven formula" for success in relationships. It might come from family and friends, self-help books and articles, or even from your therapist. You might have tried to meet Mr. or Ms. Right by socializing more, dating regularly, or honing your online profile. If you're already in a relationship, you might have practiced assertiveness and effective communication skills, as well as reminding yourself that you are worthy of love. But still, you struggle with feeling lonely and unlovable, or chronically fearing rejection. There is a reason for this; and there is a solution.

As with almost everything else in life, you learn about relationships through experience. And since your first serious relationship began as an infant with your caretakers, that is where you began learning about relationships. I know that's one of the clichés of psychology, but it's also true. Your first lessons on how available and nurturing others will be when you need them, and on how lovable you yourself are, were based on the warmth, acceptance, and reassurance offered by your parents or others who took care of you. During the early months and years of your life, you developed a certain style of connecting with—and attaching to—others.

Though you may not have been aware of this style until adolescence or adulthood (or maybe it's still unclear), your current style is probably fundamentally the same as what was nurtured in childhood. If your early experiences left you questioning your sense of being worthy of love, fearful of being rejected, or with an unquenchable thirst for reassurance, then you probably still feel this way. It could also be that painful experiences later in life intensified anxiety about relationships that previously lurked under the surface. But the basic vulnerability to this attachment-related anxiety probably developed in childhood.

It's important to understand that attachment-related anxiety does not have to be in response to any obviously abusive or harmful parenting; in fact, it most often is not. Many people with attachment-related anxiety come from very loving homes. Unfortunately, their parents' own struggles or difficult or traumatic circumstances interfered with their being able to parent effectively, even when they truly loved their children.

You might wonder, *Why would my attachment-related anxiety stubbornly stay with me through life?* To answer this, think about the practically infinite number of interactions you had with your parents or other caretakers during your childhood, day after day, year after year. (Really, stop and think about it.) These interactions—though not all of equal weight—implicitly teach you how others are likely to respond to you, and how worthy you are of being loved. Their messages layer one upon the other and fuse together, becoming part of the very fiber of your being. So, understandably, it's not easy to change—not easy, but *definitely* possible.

One important lesson that I've learned in doing therapy is that creating change is a bit like gardening. Just as a gardener doesn't reach into a seed and pull out a plant, a therapist doesn't reach into people and *make* them change. Rather, therapists provide people with what they need to grow. I listen to people, share my perceptions about them and their situation, offer compassion, and provide guidance. In response, they (hopefully) learn to see themselves differently; respond to themselves in new, more positive ways; feel encouraged to risk change (the unknown is always at least a little scary); and learn to be different. But all of this must happen at its own pace; it can be encouraged, but it cannot be forced.

One crucial element in nurturing personal growth is developing greater self-awareness. This includes being aware of your thoughts; acknowledging and consciously experiencing your emotions; and understanding what makes you tick. These tasks can be difficult, especially when you are facing unpleasant or conflicting aspects of yourself. However, they give you a better appreciation for your struggles. Such self-awareness frequently helps people feel a greater sense of well-being and, by itself, often facilitates change—such as reducing attachment-related anxiety and nurturing healthier relationships.

As important as self-awareness is, it's equally important to recognize that it occurs in the context of your relationship with yourself. And many people are too hard on themselves. Just as you would attend to a hurt child by being nurturing, it is extremely helpful to approach yourself in a compassionate manner.

Together, self-awareness and a positive relation to yourself create a powerful force, a combination I call *compassionate self-awareness*. Blended properly, they are like Miracle-Gro for the soul. Approaching your relationship struggles from this perspective is what this book is about.

Insecure in Love explains, in easy-to-understand language, how your relationship struggles first formed; what about this process makes change so hard; and how those difficulties can be overcome so that you can enjoy a secure, lasting love.

While the main thrust of this book is to help you understand what you can do to find happiness in an intimate relationship, the ideas that I present can also help you to understand your partner better. Sometimes a window into your partner's world is exactly what you need to relate to him or her more compassionately, which in turn can help you to nurture a healthier relationship.

Insecure in Love is divided into four parts. The first, "The Bedrock of All Relationships," helps you to understand your relationship struggles in the context of attachment theory. The second part, "Discover Your Potential: Being Worthy of Love," opens the door to change by helping you to identify obstacles to nurturing happy relationships. The third part, "Compassionate Self-Awareness: The Antidote to Relationship Anxiety," explains how you can develop a more secure intimate relationship with compassionate self-awareness, which is essentially being aware of your experiences while also relating to them in an accepting and compassionate manner. The fourth part, "Lighting Up Your Love Life," offers suggestions for how—with a foundation of compassionate self-awareness—you can choose a good partner and nurture a happy, healthy relationship.

Although you can read this book cover-to-cover to get an overview, I have written it as a sort of guidebook. You might even consider it a guide for a very specific kind of gardening. Remember, growth will unfold at its own pace. Your job is to enable and encourage it with fertile soil and essential nutrients. To make the most of *Insecure in Love*, read it slowly. Underline or highlight ideas you connect with. Make notes in the margins. Reread sections as necessary, perhaps even pausing in a given section to work on applying it to your life before moving on. Also, give yourself time to engage with the exercises, rather than just trying to "get them done." I strongly suggest that you keep a journal to respond to the exercises, expand on your insights, and reflect on them later. Because the chapters build on each other, I sometimes refer to exercises in previous chapters and ask you to revisit them in completing new ones.

Both my clinical practice and the research I cite are based primarily on heterosexual individuals and couples from Western cultures, so this book applies best to them. If you are from a different culture or have a different sexual orientation, you may find that you experience struggles that are beyond the scope of this book. In this case, you will still find the information on attachment styles and on developing compassionate self-awareness to be helpful, but you might want to supplement it with other relevant sources.

Finally, you will notice that throughout this book I use many examples from therapy sessions. To maintain the complete confidentiality of my patients, each example is a composite of different people and the names are fictitious.

PART ONE

The Bedrock of All Relationships

Chapter 1

Early Connections:
A Foundation for Love

To see a birth is to witness a miracle. No mother can resist wanting to hold, cuddle with, and tend to her newborn. And this is where the story of every person's life of relationships and love begins.

Infants quite literally need their caregivers for survival. So, thanks to Mother Nature, infants are hardwired with a need to connect with others, and the wherewithal to do it. For instance, they like to look at people's faces, can get others to care for them by crying, and are usually comforted by being held or rocked. And, of course, babies just look so darned cute that people want to care for them. All of this keeps their primary caregivers (usually their mothers, and secondarily their fathers) interested in protecting and nurturing them. As children become mobile, their continued need for help to survive motivates them to stay close to their mothers. A little one who ventures out will look back to Mommy for reassurance. It's in these early years, beginning with infancy, that people first learn how relationships can help them feel safe and can calm them when they are upset.

Anyone who's had experience with babies and young children has observed these behaviors, but psychoanalyst John Bowlby began publishing ideas in the late 1950s about them as signs of an attachment system. He explained that they are designed to keep a "stronger and/ or wiser" person—an *attachment figure*—close so that the child can survive and feel safe. He also offered the revolutionary notion that in order for children to thrive, their attachment figures should be warm and emotionally available (Bowlby, 1961, 1989). This idea was in direct conflict with what mothers were taught at that time. The prevailing wisdom was that a sensitive, nurturing approach to child-rearing would make children clingy and too dependent. Instead, mothers were encouraged to keep an objective, rational distance, even when their children were upset or ill (Johnson, 2008).

Bowlby's ideas were generally rejected until researcher Mary Ainsworth helped him prove the truth of his theories through her work in the 1970s, as Wallin (2007) and Mikulincer and Shaver (2007) note. Ainsworth's studies helped show that through innumerable interactions with their parents—subtle or not so subtle—children develop a way of bonding that seeps into their very being. This way of bonding becomes a *working model* that sets their expectations for how others will respond to them, as well as for how they feel about themselves. Some time later, researchers showed that the attachment process was active in romantic love (Hazan and Shaver, 1987; Feeney, 2008).

While nature provides the attachment system as a way to ensure the child's survival, attachment bonds developed within that system are felt as love—in both childhood and adulthood. So it's no surprise that children seek the love of their parents as if their lives depend on it (which they do). Adults experience similar intense anxiety and painful sadness when the existence of their primary relationships (and the love those relationships offer) feels threatened. It's also no surprise that children who tend to get upset easily and have trouble being soothed by their parents also tend to struggle with being upset easily as adults, and are unable to find a consistent, reliable sense of soothing and safety in their romantic relationships.

The Basics of How You Connect

Whom do you turn to when you are really upset? At those times, your *attachment system* is turned on; like turning on an internal homing device for which the target or "home" is an attachment figure. When an adult's system works well, he has a secure style of attachment. He seeks out his partner or other primary attachment figure for reassurance when he's upset. And once he finds her to be reliably available and effectively responsive, his attachment system turns off. He feels calm and comforted. But people with an insecure pattern of attachment don't fully or consistently find such comfort in their partners or in others, an indication that their "homing device" is malfunctioning.

Current research (Bartholomew and Horowitz, 1991) suggests that attachment styles (whether secure or insecure) are fundamentally based on two underlying "working models" (or default ways of relating)—a *working model of self* and a *working model of others*.

The working model of self is your sense of how worthy or unworthy you feel of being loved. As you might imagine, when you feel unworthy of love, you also fear being rejected and struggle with *attachment-related anxiety*. You might recognize this as anxiety—a feeling of tension or nervousness. But you could also feel it as other distressing emotions, such as sadness, loneliness, or anger. Adults and children with a strong sense of unworthiness live as though their attachment system, or homing device for an attachment figure, is stuck in the fully "on" position. If you identify with this, you may be constantly in search of reassurance from an attachment figure and chronically feel alone, rejected, or in fear of rejection. And even at the less extreme levels of attachment-related anxiety, people can struggle with feeling somewhat inadequate, and fear being unable to emotionally handle rejection. This book is designed to help you overcome such distress, whatever your level of attachment-related anxiety.

People also have a working model of others—an expectation of whether or not others will be emotionally available to them. To the extent that they expect that others won't be there for them, they feel uncomfortable with getting close and want to avoid it. This is what psychologists call *attachment-related avoidance*. There are some people who are so sure that others won't be emotionally available that they decide to be fully self-reliant. They do everything they can to try to keep themselves from feeling the need to depend on someone else. It's as if their attachment system or homing device is stuck in the "off" position.

Exercise: How Much Anxiety and Avoidance Do You Feel in Your Relationships?

To learn how much attachment-related anxiety and attachment-related avoidance you experience, consider how well you fit the paragraphs below (Ainsworth, Blehar, Water, and Wall, 1978; Simpson, Rholes, and Phillips, 1996; Collins, 1996; Feeney, Noller, and Hanrahan, 1994; Griffin and Bartholomew, 1994; Brennan, Clark, and Shaver, 1998; Levine and Heller, 2010). Rate yourself on a scale of 0–10, with 0 being not at all and 10 being that you completely relate. Hold on to these numbers so that you can use them later in assessing your attachment style.

Attachment-Related Anxiety

Being totally emotionally close with my partner means everything to me. But other people don't want to be as close as I would like to be, and my desire to be so close often scares them away. When I have a partner, I question myself and am concerned that I'm not as good as him or other people. I'm always worried that he doesn't care about me as much as I care about him. And I also worry all the time about whether my partner really loves me, will stop loving me, or will decide to leave me. I'm especially worried that he'll find someone else when we are not together.

Rating: _____

Attachment-Related Avoidance

I am an independent, self-sufficient person, so I don't need to be in a close, committed relationship. When I am in such a relationship, I prefer not to depend on my partner or to share deeply personal thoughts and feelings. And it makes me uncomfortable when my partner wants to depend on me or to talk a lot about his thoughts and feelings. When I have problems, I tend to keep them to myself and figure them out on my own, and I'd prefer it if my partner would do the same.

Rating: _____

Four Styles of Attachment

As I've explained, attachment styles can best be understood by combining the way people relate to themselves (which can create anxiety) and to others (which can result in avoidance). By dividing the dimensions of anxiety and avoidance into high and low, the following four possible combinations are created (see figure 1):

Preoccupied: High Anxiety, Low Avoidance

Fearful: High Anxiety, High Avoidance

Dismissing: Low Anxiety, High Avoidance

Secure: Low Anxiety, Low Avoidance

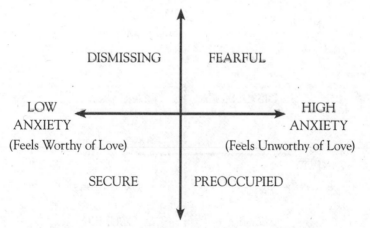

Figure 1. Four-Group Model of Attachment Styles in Adulthood. Based on Bartholomew and Horowitz (1991), Griffin and Bartholomew (1994), Mikulincer and Shaver (2007), and Levine and Heller (2010).

The original research in attachment theory labeled the attachment styles as being categorically different from each other—just as a woman and a fish are categorically different, unless you are given to believing in mermaids. However, current research research (Griffin and Bartholomew, 1994) shows that this simply isn't true. Instead, different attachment styles represent "blurry" groups that reveal tendencies, but should not be taken too literally.

Combining levels of avoidance and anxiety works a lot like mixing two primary colors. Red and yellow make orange. However, adding just a little yellow to red creates an orangey-red; and adding just a little red to yellow creates an orangey-yellow. A similar dynamic occurs with the two dimensions of attachment. Consider Ann, who is high in anxiety and *very low* in avoidance, and Dan, who is also high in anxiety but just a *little low* in avoidance. As you can see in Figure 2, both people have a preoccupied style of attachment. However, Dan is more similar to people with a fearful style.

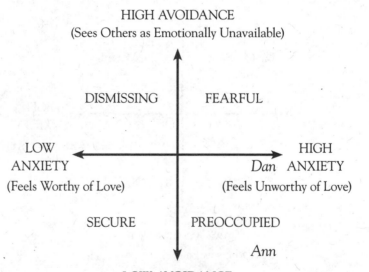

Figure 2. Dan and Ann on the Four-Group Model of Attachment Styles in Adulthood. Model based on Bartholomew and Horowitz (1991), Griffin and Bartholomew (1994), Mikulincer and Shaver (2007), and Levine and Heller (2010).

Along a similar line of thinking, you might belong more in the dismissing or secure category of attachment, but be closer to the anxious end of that grouping. In that case, you will relate to many of the struggles of anxiously attached people without actually being clearly anxiously attached. For this reason, you will also benefit from reading this book.

By understanding the "blurriness" of these groupings, you will be able to use this book more effectively. It is tempting to assess your style of attachment and then pigeonhole yourself. For instance, you might think of yourself as having a preoccupied or fearful attachment style. However, you would not be taking all aspects of *you*—the unique person that you are—into account. The best way to reduce your relationship anxiety and improve yourself is based largely on self-understanding. So when you read about the four attachment styles, think about *how much* you relate to each one, not just which category you fit in.

It's also important to recognize that your attachment style can change with experience. For instance, consider Heather. She had always felt inadequate as a person, and exhibited a preoccupied attachment style. Her husband, Alan, reinforced this feeling with his frequent focus on her mistakes and shortcomings. He eventually divorced her, leaving her to struggle even more with a deeper sense of being unlovable. But with therapy she began seriously questioning this negative view of herself. For instance, she was able to realize that Alan had been overly critical. Then she met Sam, who valued her thoughtfulness and creativity. She basked in his love and warmth, which melted her remaining self-rejection and helped her to feel more comfortable with being valued by someone else. Romantic relationships often serve as a special opportunity for you to revise your attachment style so as to be healthier—an opportunity that this book can help you to realize.

In addition to assessing your own style of attachment, think about the other styles, too. Consider the styles of your current or past partners, or even your friends and colleagues. Your attachment-related anxiety can prompt you to make quick, and often inaccurate, emotional judgments of others. As a result, you might misunderstand your partner's emotions, struggles, and behaviors. This can cause significant problems in your relationship. By understanding your partner's attachment style better, you can understand him and the dynamics between the two of you better. Also, by having a good grasp of secure attachment, you can understand the benefits of working toward this for yourself and you can understand how having a securely attached partner can help you.

One last important caveat before you read about the attachment styles: A simple reading of these styles will leave you with the impression that the only "good" way to have a healthy relationship is to have a secure attachment style. This impression would be wrong. The "best" way to attach is to have a romantic relationship that makes you happy. If you tend toward having a preoccupied style of attachment and are married to someone who also has that tendency, but the two of you are happy—then trust in that. Enjoy it. Your style and life circumstance are right for you. As it happens, one significant way (but not the only way) of finding happiness in your relationship when you are unhappy is to move toward a more secure style. But as you evaluate your life and what you might want to change, it is important that you keep your eye on the real "prize": happiness in love.

Secure Attachment: Happy in Love

Sue is basically a happy person. She loves her work as an elementary school teacher and thinks of herself as very good at it. In her off hours she enjoys playing tennis and hiking with two of her close girlfriends. She is also happily engaged to Keith, whom she unhesitatingly trusts and relies on for support. Of course, no relationship is perfect. For instance, there was the time when he stood her up for dinner because he forgot about their plans: in the immortal words of Ricky Ricardo, he had "lots of 'splainin' to do." But even in that sort of situation, when she gets angry with him, they are able to talk through their problems and she ends up feeling that he really cares.

Like approximately 60 percent of people, Sue is securely attached. Securely attached individuals are basically comfortable with their full range of emotions and feel like lovable, good, caring, competent people. They are also inclined to think of their partners as trustworthy, well-intentioned, sensitive, and emotionally there for them. So they are happy with themselves and in their relationships.

Just as they are comfortable with their relationships in general, securely attached people are also happy with their sex lives. Placing a high priority on emotional intimacy, they tend to remain faithful, feel comfortable discussing sex, and enjoy the pleasures that it has to offer.

If you are anxiously attached and fortunate enough to have a securely attached partner, then you will find this stable and positive way of relating to be comforting, providing an opportunity for you to develop a more secure attachment style.

Preoccupied Attachment: Desperate for Love

Meet Rachel—someone you might relate to, if only a little bit. She looks to her boyfriend, Phil, to reassure her that she is worthy of love because she is unsure of this. But when he is affectionate and shows interest in her, she doesn't know what to think because it doesn't fit with her self-perceptions. She constantly worries about how much Phil really cares about her. She's sure that once he gets to know "the real me," he'll immediately leave her. So she constantly worries that he won't want to get together with her on the weekends. And whenever he doesn't respond immediately to her texts, she assumes he's avoiding her. This looming possibility of rejection is overwhelming, and so she is preoccupied with that fear.

People like Rachel who have a preoccupied attachment style are sensitive to the possibility of being overlooked or rejected by their partner, whom they need to protect them. So they use *hyperactivating strategies* to keep their attachment system "turned on" (or activated), which ensures that they will continue to seek out a reliable attachment figure. For instance, they often overreact to problems and underestimate their ability to cope; they might also constantly scan for possible problems in the past, present, and future. In creating all of these negative feelings and thoughts, they heighten their need for an attachment figure and are essentially crying out for one. Unfortunately, those who do this to an extreme can also end up feeling chronically overwhelmed, vulnerable, and needy.

Their sensitivity to any possible signs of rejection unintentionally instigates fights and creates distance in their intimate relationships.

It's a given that at some point their partners *will* misunderstand them, be physically unavailable, or not respond in a caring enough manner; but people with preoccupied attachment styles will view this with alarm. A clear example of this is how upset Rachel becomes when Phil doesn't immediately respond to her texts. Although people with a pre-occupied style might begin a relationship feeling intoxicated by their new love, they often quickly get caught up in their own distress. Then they are apt to see their partners as unloving (or not consistently available), untrustworthy, and possibly unfaithful. This leads to them being possessive and unrealistically jealous. To make matters worse, they are often unable to calm down enough to forgive their partners for any wrongdoing. So their relationships are unstable and easily disrupted by problems. As a result, people like Rachel are usually unhappy in love.

Because their attachment needs and struggles feel so strong, some people with a preoccupied attachment style organize their lives around trying to prove that they are worthy of love, or trying to distract themselves from their negative feelings. This interferes with their ability to express themselves in an authentic way or to pursue personal interests. Rachel, for example, did very well in college, but settled for a job as a receptionist after graduation—and remained in it for years—because she couldn't decide what to do with her bachelor's degree in English. She was also constantly worried at work about what others thought of her performance. Although it didn't go quite this far with Rachel, people with a preoccupied style often carry their issues and unhappiness from home into work. In addition, the constant stress and anxiety that they feel often causes health problems.

Just as they do with the rest of their lives, people with a preoccupied attachment style approach their sex lives with a drive to gain reassurance and avoid rejection. So although they often enjoy being held and caressed without really wanting more sexual intimacy, they turn to sex to get the assurance and acceptance that they seek. Men, in their attempts to feel loved and accepted by a woman, tend to be more sexually reserved and to look for their partner to be sexually responsive and pleased. By contrast, women, in their attempts to feel loved and accepted by a man, tend to be less reserved, or sometimes promiscuous. In both cases, they often struggle with feeling that their partners or situations control their sex lives, and they are often uncomfortable talking with their partners about sex.

Dismissing Attachment: No Need for Love

Now, meet Andy. Think about whether you relate to him at all, or whether he sounds like anyone you know. He is proud of his independence, his self-sufficiency, and his commitment to his sales job. He enjoyed spending time with his ex-girlfriend, Chris, but he wasn't too upset when she ended their relationship. To him, she made too big a deal of his business trips by wanting him to call her, though she only asked for an occasional check-in. He also felt she wanted to talk about her feelings and their relationship "all the time." So now he's happy not to have to take care of her. Although he sometimes feels left out when his friends are talking about their girlfriends, he says he's not bothered by it and actually prefers to spend the time alone. What Andy denies, even to himself, is that he actively minimizes and avoids his feelings. This is very characteristic of people with a dismissing attachment style, and it places them at risk for anxiety and depression.

Like those with a preoccupied style, those with a dismissing style are also prone to believe that their partners will not reliably be there to support or comfort them. But they protect themselves by unconsciously using *deactivating strategies* that "turn off" (or deactivate) their attachment system, enabling them to avoid being in the untenable position of feeling a pull to rely on an undependable partner. They effectively suppress, avoid, or ignore their emotions and attachment needs. They tend to remain distant, limit their interactions and intimate conversations, and frequently denigrate their partners. For example, while Andy often seemed kind as he helped Chris with her finances, which she appreciated, this also allowed him to remain in a distant and superior position, which only increased her negative feelings about herself. At other times, Andy would keep a safe distance and respond to Chris's attempts to be emotionally intimate by telling her that she was "just too needy." This, of course, only increased her self-doubts. In the end, dismissing people might truly care about their partners, but they do so without getting too intimate or emotionally entangled.

Generally unaware of their feelings, dismissing people aren't fully equipped to cope with emotionally upsetting experiences. For instance, when their partners aggravate them, they try to minimize or deny their anger. However, that anger continues to exist under the surface, often making them tense and unforgiving. This dynamic, of course, does not bode well for their relationships; but it can't be easily addressed or rectified because so much of it occurs outside of their awareness. This dynamic is most problematic for anxiously attached partners, who tend to interpret the dismissing partner's anger as evidence that there is something wrong with them.

So why doesn't the dismissing partner just leave? Even those with a dismissing style need comfort and connection. So they seek out and stay in romantic relationships, even as they simultaneously protect themselves by being excessively self-sufficient in those relationships.

Dismissing people approach their sexualities in the same distant and self-protective way as they engage in relationships in general. Because physical or sexual contact can weaken their defenses, many are uncomfortable with connecting through touch, such as with hugs or gentle caressing. They might abstain from sex, sometimes choosing to rely on masturbation. Or they might remain emotionally distant by limiting sex to one-night stands or short-term relationships that are only superficially close. When they are in intimate relationships, they tend not to be affectionate and may be emotionally disengaged during sex. This can leave anxious partners feeling unattractive and unworthy of love.

Fearful Attachment: Conflicted in Love

John describes himself as an emotional mess. He has been this way since he was a kid. By the age of fourteen, he was essentially taking care of himself because his father was an angry drunk and his mother was busy trying to hold the family together while working long hours. He thinks of himself as flawed, needy, helpless, and unworthy of love. And he believes that others know something is wrong with him and therefore keep their distance. So although he would love a committed, romantic relationship, he avoids getting close out of fear that he'll be rejected or misunderstood.

This conflict between an intense fear of rejection and a desperate need for reassurance and closeness is typical of people with a fearful attachment style. When they are not totally avoiding relationships, they end up behaving in contradictory and confusing ways. Prone to seeing partners as emotionally distant, they sometimes try desperately to get their partners' approval and attention by using hyperactivating strategies such as exaggerating their distress. However, when they perceive their partners as getting close, they feel vulnerable to getting hurt. So they instinctively look to protect themselves from their partner, turning to deactivating strategies to avoid intimacy. In John's case, he would spend his weekends repairing old furniture, limiting the time he could be with his girlfriend (when he had one). This constant tension between being too close or too distant leaves fearfully attached people chronically distressed, insecure, extremely passive, and emotionally distant. Not surprisingly, they are at high risk for anxiety, depression, and other emotional struggles.

Convinced that their partners are emotionally unavailable, fearfully attached people tend to view their partners in a particularly negative light and have trouble empathizing with them. For instance, when John was dating Amanda and would meet her after work for dinner, he would invariably conclude she was uninterested in him when she was really just tired from a long day. This predisposition, of course, creates tension in relationships. But those with a fearful style are likely to just stew in their feelings rather than directly address them. Probably because of their sense that they are unworthy of love, they tend to remain in their relationships even when those relationships are seriously troubled or even abusive. On the other hand, because of their discomfort with intimacy and being appreciated (though it's what they desperately want), they are likely to feel something is wrong and end a relationship, even when they are in love and their partner is truly caring.

Just as they struggle with being emotionally intimate with their partners, they also struggle with being physically intimate. Sometimes this means using casual sex as a way of remaining emotionally distant and safe while also trying to meet their need for comfort, acceptance, and reassurance. They might do this with one-night stands or short-term relationships (that end when they start feeling vulnerable). When they are less focused on meeting their attachment needs and are more in the mode of protecting themselves, they are likely to avoid sexual intimacy and its accompanying vulnerability.

Discovering Your Attachment Style

If you have not already done so, review the four styles of attachment and decide which one you most resemble. But remember, you are unlikely to fit any one style to a T. So pay attention to how your personal attachment style incorporates some of the characteristics of the other styles. For instance, are you basically secure but with a tendency toward doubting your self-worth (being preoccupied)? Also keep in mind that although you have a particular, characteristic style, it will likely vary a bit with different relationships.

Another way you can assess your style of attachment is to graph your ratings on the dimensions of anxiety and avoidance. Get a clean sheet of paper. (Graph paper is best, if you have it.) Draw a horizontal line and label it *Anxiety*. Place evenly spaced tic marks along it, numbering them from 0 to 10 (from left to right). Then, at the 5, draw a vertical line and label it *Avoidance*. Again, place evenly spaced tic marks along it and number them from 0 to 10 (from bottom to top, placing the 5 where this line crosses the horizontal line). Now you have a graph that looks like figure 1. Copy the style descriptions from figure 1 into each of the quadrants on your graph. To determine your rating for attachment-related anxiety and attachment-related avoidance, look back to the exercise "How Much Anxiety and Avoidance Do You Feel in Your Relationships?" Using your two ratings, plot where you fall in the quadrants and place a dot there. Not only will you see the style quadrant into which you fall, but you will also see how close you are to each of the other quadrants. The less extreme you are on each of the dimensions, the less your traits will match the prototypical style of the quadrant that you are in.

A third way of determining your attachment style in intimate relationships is to use an online survey (including the empirically validated "Experiences in Close Relationships—Revised" questionnaire) developed by researcher Chris Fraley and colleagues (Fraley, Vicary, Brumbaugh, and Roisman, 2011). You can find a link to this questionnaire on my website: http://www.drbecker-phelps.com/insecure.html. Along with revealing your attachment style, it also shows where you fall on a graph of attachment-related anxiety and attachment-related avoidance.

Once you are clear about your own attachment style, you might want to look at the attachment style of your partner or past partners. You can rate them the same way you rated yourself, using your observations about them and their behaviors. You can also have current partners rate themselves if they are open to it; the advantage of this is that it can open some illuminating and intimacy-building conversations. In both cases, understanding their style of attachment will help you to better understand them and the relationship the two of you have or had.

Finally, knowing your attachment style is an effective first step to changing it. So you've already accomplished a lot just by getting to this point. Understanding how your style developed is also important. And this is what I'll discuss next.

Chapter 2

Understanding Why You Relate the Way You Do

My goal in this chapter is to clarify the development of attachment styles well enough that you can look at yourself (and your partner) and honestly say, "Well, of course you're struggling with that. The ways you are thinking and feeling make perfect sense." As with any problem, the first step toward a solution is to approach it with a positive attitude and true understanding.

To start, it's essential that you understand the attachment system's three basic functions:

Proximity: People naturally strive to keep their attachment figure (usually a parent or romantic partner) close.

Safe haven: When people feel threatened, they look to an attachment figure for protection, comfort, and support.

Secure base: When people feel safe and supported around an attachment figure, they feel freer to pursue goals apart from that relationship.

Your experience in adult relationships is very much related to how well each of these functions was met by caregivers during your childhood, and how well they've been met by attachment figures in subsequent relationships. No, you can't blame it all on your parents. But a healthy, informed look back can go a long way toward putting you on the road to healthier relationships, by clarifying where you came from.

Proximity: Protection from Danger

The safety of young children is dependent on caregivers being close and attentive. Even as children mature into adolescence and young adulthood, they still rely on their parents, though the parent-child relationship changes significantly. They broaden their network of attachment figures and so might also rely on other family members, mentors, clergy, or close friends. And then, significantly, they often look to a romantic partner (eventually a spouse) as their principal attachment figure to help them feel safe and to support their interests.

However, "closeness" means something a bit different for an adult than for a young child. Adults are more effective in using *mental representations*, or images, of attachment figures for a sense of comfort. This means that *thinking* of your partner, parent, or close friend can give you the sense that they are emotionally close, which allows you to symbolically return to them as a safe haven and a secure base. Over time, you might come to identify so much with certain caregivers that you incorporate their way of relating to you into yourself, enabling you to maintain a sense that you have value and to generally expect that others will be supportive. Unfortunately, the more you struggle with attachment-related anxiety, the less likely you are to truly believe that you have value or that others value you. As a result, you will have more difficulty using mental representations as a safe haven to self-soothe or as a secure base for exploration.

(I will return to the idea of mental representations later in the book, because developing them is crucial to lessening your anxiety and distress in relationships.)

Safe Haven: The Need for Comfort

Children are biologically wired to look to their parents as a safe haven from threats. For instance, many young children run to their parents for protection during loud thunderstorms or when they meet a clown at the circus (which, from their perspective, is an understandably scary creature). However, it's not enough for parents to offer physical safety. Children must *feel* safe and comforted in their parents' presence.

Parents who can maintain their emotional equilibrium do the best job of this. By not getting caught up in their own emotions, they are free to have empathy for their children's experiences right from infancy. When children feel that their parents empathize with and respect their experiences, they feel good about themselves and their developing abilities. As the children mature, these parents continue to provide sensitive responses as a way to help them accept, understand, and cope with their emotions. (Keep in mind that no parent is perfectly consistent or in tune with her child. Rather than being perfect, caregivers only need to be what psychoanalyst Donald Winnicott [1953] calls "good enough.")

Unfortunately, not all parents are able to do this—even when they love their children. As a result, their children do not experience a reliable safe haven. They don't feel fully accepted, and might not feel worthy of love. They might also view their parents (and by extension, others) as emotionally unavailable and unsupportive. These experiences of self and others persist into adulthood. (And, as you might remember from chapter 1, experiences of self and experiences of others are the two working models that underlie attachment styles.) So to the extent that childhood caretakers were inconsistent or unavailable in providing you with a safe haven, you will likely be preoccupied with the fear of your partner leaving you; or you might just not even look to your partner for comfort.

To enjoy a secure and happy relationship, you need to face your fears of being unlovable and rejected, understand them, and nurture a new sense of having a safe haven in your adult relationships. It's not an easy task, but it is definitely doable. To help you face and understand this struggle better, complete the next exercise.

Exercise: Looking for a Safe Haven in Your Relationship

How sensitive are you to either physical or emotional separations? When your partner is doing something outside of your relationship, how do you feel about it? Are you quick to feel abandoned, rejected, or just not cared about? If so, allow yourself to experience, acknowledge, and explore your reactions (for example, feeling painfully alone or vulnerable). Remember that whatever your reactions are, they have their basis in an attachment system that was evolved to keep you safe from harm. The intensity of your feelings is your attachment system's way of calling out, "Hey, I need help here! If you aren't here for me, I might die!"

If you are fortunate enough not to feel particularly sensitive to separations, consider what you do feel. How much are you comforted by a sense of your partner being with you (or by a sense of being part of a couple) even when you are physically apart? Or do you *not* feel comforted even when he is around? Consider whether you feel—or try to feel—detached so that you are relatively immune from being hurt by your partner. Take time to think about situations when you and your partner have been away from each other, and explore your reactions to them.

♡

Secure Base: Support for Exploring the World

In addition to offering a safe haven in times of trouble, attachment figures also provide children with a secure base from which they can expand their experience. This is important because people are born with an innate desire to learn about and master their environment. When children successfully get support for this, they gradually become more independent and develop a sense of autonomy, an ability to act from their own inherent interests and values—for instance, a preschooler will curiously explore an unfamiliar playroom or reach out to a kid they don't know on the playground.

To develop a secure base, children need to feel loved for who they are and for who they are becoming. They need to learn that tensions and differences in interest with their parents can all be worked through. In this process, children also learn that they can explore and venture apart from their parents, and still rely on them for support and acceptance.

To the extent that people are fortunate enough to have a secure base in their parents, they develop high self-esteem and a strong sense of autonomy that will serve them well through life. They are more likely to pursue their interests, be persistent in their efforts, and do well at school and work. In their romantic relationships, they tend to feel connected with, and supported by, their partners as they pursue their own interests. And more generally, they tend to enjoy healthy relationships and can effectively negotiate social situations. But this isn't the case for everyone.

If you experience at least a fair amount of attachment-related anxiety, reading these benefits of a secure base might highlight some of your intense struggles—such as a failure to explore (or even identify) your own interests and passions, and a hesitancy to express yourself with your partner. As hard as it is to feel this distress, you're already working on it just by being aware of how you would benefit from having a secure base. Later, in parts 3 and 4 of this book, I will guide you toward ways to develop greater security within yourself and your relationships.

Balancing Autonomy and Closeness

To recap the previous few sections: Children are motivated to stay close to their parents, whom they perceive as a safe haven. And children are motivated to explore the world away from their parents, whom they perceive as a secure base. When all goes well, children learn that they can have closeness *and* autonomy.

Your struggles with attachment-related anxiety can cloud your perception of these patterns in your relationships and make it particularly frustrating to understand what's going wrong. To help clarify this, I will discuss how people with the different insecure patterns of attachment balance autonomy and closeness. As you read the following sections, think about how they apply to you, your partner, and your relationship.

Preoccupied: Grasping for Closeness

Some children perceive their parents as inconsistently available. It could be because the parents are unavoidably focused on pressing life situations or on their own emotional needs. The child's inherent sensitivity is also a factor. Whatever the reason, children who come to question whether their parents are available are extremely upset even by the thought of their parents not being there for them. This is characteristic of a preoccupied attachment style.

Driven by their attachment needs, such children do whatever they can to get their parents' attention—and, as adults, to get their partner's attention. These *protests*, as John Bowlby (1961), the originator of attachment theory, called them, are a hyperactivating strategy. That is, anxious people "hyperactivate" their attachment system as their cries for attention become more strident, making them more upset and often causing conflict in their relationships. For instance, they might demand that their partner help them in various ways, try to maintain constant contact, or become easily jealous and possessive.

PROTESTS AGAINST POSSIBLE ABANDONMENT	
Being needy	Being in frequent need of your partner's help for particular tasks or for emotional comfort.
Reestablishing communication	Constantly calling or texting. Trying to create situations where you will run into your partner.
Maintaining physical contact	Excessively hugging, kissing, and being physically intimate to avoid separation.
Game playing	Trying to make your partner jealous by pretending someone else is interested in you. Being distant to entice your partner to reach out. Pretending to share interests and values.

Expressing anger directly	Speaking to your partner in a nasty tone or with condescension. Physically expressing anger with facial expressions or even hitting your partner.
Expressing anger indirectly	Rebuffing your partner by walking away. Giving your partner the "cold shoulder." Not returning calls, texts, or e-mails.

People with preoccupied attachment needs focus intensely on keeping others close, at the expense of their own interests and sometimes even their values. This leaves them empty, without an experience of themselves that they feel good about. Instead, they look to someone else, such as a parent, friend, or spouse, for approval and guidance on what interests to pursue and how to respond to various circumstances. They are also often motivated by external, image-oriented goals (such as financial wealth) as a way to receive approval. Unfortunately, this search for external approval keeps them forever performing, which gets in the way of their feeling truly accepted by an attachment figure. Thus, they are frequently left without the sense of closeness they crave and without a positive sense of themselves, and are incapable of pursuing their own interests.

Dismissing: Making It on Your Own

While some children are preoccupied with trying to get and keep their parents' attention, others give up trying to connect. As Bowlby (1961) explained, after a child's protests go repeatedly unanswered, or are mostly responded to harshly, the child experiences despair. Then, when he finally gives up all hope of being reassured and protected, he detaches—attempting to deactivate his attachment system by shutting down his emotions and his need for a caregiver—and becomes extremely self-reliant. As an adult, he is unlikely to experience the closeness that comes with romantic relationships. This characterizes the dismissing style of attachment.

If your partner tends toward a dismissing style, you might feel confused when he distances himself, rather than softening, in response to your reaching out in a supportive way. The reason for this reaction is that he will not risk being let down later; so he retreats and may become even more distant. Similarly, when you are upset with your partner, he is likely to appear emotionally disengaged and unbothered. In all likelihood, however, he fears being rejected.

Dismissive people lose out on two fronts. Unable to act on their desire for connection, they are neither truly autonomous nor capable of feeling close to a partner.

Fearful: Lost in Relationships

Some children grow up with parents who have their own strong attachment issues: they experience their parents as sometimes emotionally available, sometimes scared, and sometimes even scary. This variation is confusing and frightening, and these children are unable to find a way to consistently meet their attachment needs. They don't find solace in either deactivating (trying to go it alone) or hyperactivating (reaching out for attention and acceptance), so they attempt to use both kinds of strategies in a disorganized way. This creates a chaotic and confusing pattern in relationships known as the fearful style of attachment. In adulthood, their intimate relationships are often filled with conflict and confusing dynamics, as they pursue both closeness and distance. Not surprisingly, they are not able to achieve a comfortable and comforting sense of closeness or a healthy sense of autonomy.

Exercise: How Well Do You Balance Autonomy and Closeness?

Relationships are, of course, more of an ongoing, dynamic balancing act than achieving some continuously held equilibrium. With that in mind, which of the following pictures *best* represents your ideal relationship? And which picture best represents your current relationship, or your most recent one?

 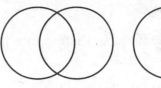 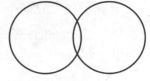

Anxious Style   Secure Style   Avoidant Style

These styles are expressed in the following statements:

Secure Style:

- I am comfortable sharing intimate thoughts and feelings with my partner.

- I enjoy pursuing interests apart from my partner.

- I feel loved by my partner even when we pursue interests separately from each other.

- Even when we disagree, I expect that my partner will still respect and value my opinions and me.

- I am comfortable depending on my partner and having my partner depend on me.

Anxious Style:

- I am most comfortable when my partner and I share all of our thoughts, feelings, and interests—when we seem to have merged into one.

- I am inclined to pursue what my partner enjoys, putting aside my own interests.

- I am inclined to defer my values and opinions to my partner's values and opinions.

- Whenever I sense my partner being distant, I feel driven to reconnect (for example, frequently calling or texting); or I act angrily, such as by withdrawing or being nasty.

Avoidant Style:

- I am uncomfortable sharing intimate thoughts and feelings with my partner.

- I take pride in being self-reliant enough not to need my partner.

- I am uncomfortable depending on my partner.

- I am uncomfortable with my partner depending on me.

- I enjoy pursuing interests apart from my partner.

In doing this exercise, you might want to draw your own overlapping circles and write your own descriptive sentences that better depict your relationship. (We humans are complicated, so it's okay if your description includes conflicting sentences.)

Now consider how well your relationship meets your needs for a:

Safe haven: During stressful times, how much can you depend on your partner to provide you with a sense of comfort, protection, and support?

Secure base: How much does your partner support your pursuit of interests and goals apart from your relationship? How well does your relationship support your feeling good about your true sense of who you are?

Managing Your Emotions

During infancy, children are practically swimming in emotions. Their interactions with their parents are strongly guided by their basic goal of survival and their accompanying need to feel secure. A part of their brain called the amygdala is particularly sensitive to threats to their safety. It is quick to react to possible dangers, such as hunger, being alone, or falling. It reacts reflexively, without evaluating dangers and adjusting its reaction based on the real threat. When you are walking in the woods and feel a rush of fear at the sight of a stick that you mistake as a snake, you can thank your amygdala. Modulating this response is the function of the hippocampus, but that part of the brain doesn't begin to work until children are between two and three years old. Until then, all dangers are perceived equally and trigger a desperate search for a safe attachment figure to protect and soothe them. This feeling is what neuroscientist Jaak Panksepp refers to as *primal panic* (referenced in Johnson, 2008); and it continues to be triggered into adulthood whenever people feel threatened. It also frequently kicks in when they fear losing their partner or other primary attachment figure.

Depending on your attachment style, you will feel primal panic more or less often; and you will be more or less effective in managing it. The same is true of your partner, if you have one. The result of these different experiences has a huge impact on your relationship. In the next three sections I discuss how the anxious, avoidant, and secure attachment styles affect people's emotional experiences and how they manage those experiences.

Anxious and Overwhelmed

When a child experiences primal panic, it raises her levels of the stress hormones adrenaline and cortisol. At the same time, it also lowers her "cuddle hormone" oxytocin, which provides a sense of trust, safety, and connection. Feeling overwhelmed, she reacts by protesting—crying, or being demanding. In essence, she is screaming for help. If her caregiver is inconsistent in soothing her, she remains primed to protest—to keep screaming for help until she gets it. This tendency characterizes those who are anxiously attached.

In its extreme form, these children mature into adults who are prone to panic at any hint of distance from their partner, and possibly even others, such as family and friends. They become desperate to feel close to the other party again and try to regain their partner's attention by intensifying their distress (a hyperactivating strategy). But even with a supportive partner, their fear of rejection can interfere with their feeling comforted.

If you can even somewhat relate to this, you might also sometimes find it hard to disentangle your emotions. Instead, you perceive them as a single distressing experience that you cannot begin to communicate or address. In an effort to cope with this, you might fall back on maladaptive behaviors, such as overeating, smoking, drinking, or even drug use.

When attachment-related anxiety is a problem, people experience a number of other problems in their relationships that you might relate to. For instance, your fear of rejection might prevent you from directly addressing any conflicts or differences of opinion with your partner. It might also be so consuming that you are unable to imagine the world (or your relationship) through your partner's eyes. As a result, you might have trouble feeling empathic and supportive of your partner (or others). In addition, you might have trouble truly relaxing enough to fully enjoy other aspects of your relationship, such as your sexual desires—and just having fun.

When relationships don't work out, people with attachment-related anxiety can experience a need for an attachment figure that's so intense that it practically seeps out of their pores. They may protest angrily, blame themselves, feel a greater attraction to their former partner, and even become preoccupied with that partner, despite knowing that a relationship with that person is destructive for them. In addition, they can struggle with feeling that they've lost a part of themselves.

Fortunately, if you are sometimes overwhelmed with attachment-related anxiety, you can change this. In chapter 5 I discuss how to develop a more secure style. Also, you can soothe your distress by choosing a more secure partner; someone who can comfort you. Research suggests that a supportive spouse can help an anxiously attached person feel less anxious and depressed, and feel greater satisfaction in her relationship.

Exercise: Can You Relate to "Anxious and Overwhelmed"?

Think about how much and in what ways you relate to the use of the hyperactivating strategies described in this section. Be aware that fully exploring this could take you months (or even years). But, for now, I'm just suggesting that you explore the following questions as much—or as little—as you'd like in order to gain some understanding of how your attachment style affects your emotions. If you do not have a partner now, think about it in relation to a previous partner. You might also find it helpful to identify and highlight a pattern by thinking about how these questions apply to all of your previous intimate relationships.

1. *Do you frequently feel that your partner is emotionally distant, or worry that he or she will leave you? Does this thought make you feel crushed and desperate to keep your partner close (primal panic)?*

2. *Even though you might not do it consciously, can you see how you protest against being left alone? What are examples of this?*

3. *Protests often backfire, causing people to feel more upset or overwhelmed. For each example you gave, explain how it made you feel and possibly even led to more distress.*

4. *Do you struggle with feeling helpless, incompetent, or flawed? Think about how your attachment style and protests are related to this.*

5. *For some people, being overly emotional leads to maladaptive ways of coping, such as smoking, drinking, using drugs, or overeating. Do you have maladaptive ways of coping? How have they been a problem for you?*

6. *How does your panic about being left alone (if you do panic) influence your relationship in unhealthy ways, such as by*

creating conflicts around trust and—purposefully or subconsciously—making it difficult for you to relax and enjoy your partner's company?

Emotions? What Emotions?

Children with a more avoidant style of attachment block their emotional reactions to threats, including their primal panic about the unavailability of caretakers. With time, they learn to keep their attachment system deactivated, and they no longer try to connect with their parents or struggle with separation. Later in their lives, they are similarly disconnected from their partners.

It's important to understand that the tendency to distance oneself from emotions does not prevent emotions or physiological arousal. It only obscures them. Stress hormones still surge while oxytocin ("cuddle hormone") levels remain low. So, although ignoring, suppressing, or denying emotions can often help to handle minor stressors, this approach is seriously flawed.

When people with avoidant attachment styles can no longer ignore their feelings because their stress or relationship problems have become so severe and persistent, they often don't know how to handle their emotions. This puts them at risk for using unhealthy ways to cope. Their emotions are also likely to leak out despite their apparently calm demeanor. For instance, an avoidant man might calmly talk about his girlfriend being "such a bitch," all the while denying any anger, unaware that his chest is tight and his heart rate is up. You might consider whether this common dynamic is what's going on when you think you are calm but are uncharacteristically saying or doing hurtful things. (If your partner tends to be the avoidant one, this dynamic might also explain why you are upset at times when your partner seems to be calmly talking about serious problems.)

The Chemistry of "Secure and Happy"

Some children are fortunate enough to have parents who consistently nurture and calm them when they get upset. The more this happens, the better they learn to turn to their parents—and the more they produce the hormone oxytocin, which gives them a sense of trust, safety, and connection. When children (and adults) are upset, oxytocin also brings down their levels of stress hormones, adrenaline and cortisol. Over time, these responses help them to become comfortable with the full range of their emotions and integrate them into their lives. They grow to be securely attached adults who are capable of managing their own emotions, addressing personal problems, and effectively dealing with conflicts.

It can be heartening to learn that, as an anxiously attached person, you can "earn" secure attachment—along with all of its benefits. This is something I will address more later in this chapter. You can also lessen your attachment-related anxiety and other distress by choosing a securely attached partner.

Exercise: Understanding Yourself in Context

The better you understand how your hyperactivating or deactivating strategies developed, the more appreciation you will have for why you do what you do now. As you complete this exercise, be patient with yourself. Deepening self-understanding in this area can be nurtured, but it cannot be forced to happen all at once. So you may need to revisit this repeatedly over time.

Make note of when you use hyperactivating or deactivating strategies. Return to your responses for the previous exercise, "Can You Relate to "Anxious and Overwhelmed"?" Think about them—maybe even talk with someone you trust about them. Make sure you have a good grasp of your use of hyperactivating strategies.

If you regularly use deactivating strategies to keep a distance, you may have trouble being specific about how you do this because you are likely out of touch with your feelings. In that case, I suggest that you look for feedback from people you trust and who know you well. Ask them about what you do to distance people.

Consider whether you used these same, or similar, strategies as a child. If you did, then think about what might have prompted you to do this. Sometimes you can gain insight about this by considering another child in that same situation.

Example: Jane's last two boyfriends told her, "You are just too needy." Although she complained that neither of them was very affectionate, she also knew they were right. She was constantly afraid that they were going to end the relationship, so she would incessantly call and text them, looking for reassurance that they still cared. When she considered this dynamic, she realized that it reminded her of how she felt when she was eight years old and her father died. From then on, she had always been afraid of getting close to people, because she feared they would leave her.

Again, don't expect a deeper self-awareness to appear overnight. Journal, make notes, and talk with trusted people about this exercise. But also give it a rest; then return to it again after you feel you've had a chance to grow personally and have perhaps become open to new insights and perspectives. With time, a greater understanding of your patterns can help you to manage your feelings differently, both within yourself and in your relationships.

Two Ways to Earn Security and Happy Relationships

To nurture a healthier way of connecting in romantic relationships, consider how your current or future relationship might be better if you had a more secure style of attachment. As you think about this, however, it's important for you to know that you do not need to be the model of secure attachment to find happiness. But whatever style works for you, it will probably need to be closer to a secure one on the attachment-related anxiety and attachment-related avoidance dimensions. Fortunately, as I've mentioned, you can develop this more secure style as an adult. This process is what psychologists call "earned security."

There are two basic pathways, and they intertwine. First, you must look to the outside world. You need to begin by developing a relationship with at least one emotionally available attachment figure. If not a partner, then you can start with someone else, such as a family member, friend, clergyperson, or therapist. It could even be God. Remember, attachment figures are those you feel you can turn to in times of distress and who are supportive of your attempts to expand your personal horizons. The more you experience feeling accepted and protected, the more you will believe that you are worthy of love and that capable others can be available to truly love and comfort you—giving you some "earned security."

The second approach to developing "earned security" is to directly nurture a part of yourself that makes you more aware of your experiences *and* to respond to those experiences in a more accepting and compassionate way. I will explain in chapter 5 how together, as compassionate self-awareness, these two processes can help you open up to reassurance and acceptance by others, to feel their support even when you are alone (as mental representations of attachment figures), and to essentially be an available attachment figure to yourself.

The path to healthier relationships includes a more positive relationship both with yourself and with others. Teaching you how to achieve this is what the rest of this book is about. To start, I'll help you to see more clearly how you perpetuate your current attachment style in everyday life—and what's prevented you from choosing a healthier path.

PART TWO

Discover Your Potential: Being Worthy of Love

Chapter 3

Opening the Door
to Change

Each morning, you look in the mirror with the sense that you know exactly who's staring back at you. Rather than having to continually rediscover yourself—the high value you place on books and learning, or your preference for vanilla ice cream—you just *know* who you are. This is your identity, and you rely on it to support you each day just as you rely on the ground beneath your feet.

When you're not confident about important parts of your identity—as is often the case with anxiously attached people—it leads to self-doubt. In addition, the more strongly you identify with some aspect of your personality, the more motivated you are to interpret your actions from that perspective and then continue to behave accordingly. As a result, your self-doubt or sense of inadequacy can drive you to be indecisive and self-deprecating. Although your self-perceptions and actions leave you feeling negatively toward yourself, you continue the cycle because at least it allows you to feel safe in being able to understand yourself and what you think you need from others.

It is equally important that you have a sense of predictability about the identities of other people. Imagine what it would be like to have no idea of whether each person you meet is the equivalent of Mother Teresa or Jack the Ripper. And so people tend to hold beliefs about others, rightly or wrongly, based on certain characteristics—man or woman, Caucasian or Hispanic, white-collar or blue-collar worker. On an even more basic level, we all have beliefs about human nature. For example, some believe that humans tend to be altruistic, while others believe that most people they meet are self-centered. Such beliefs guide the way we approach all relationships—from casual to intimate ones. For instance, you would probably invite a new friend to your home sooner if you are someone who believes that people are basically good rather than someone who tends to doubt people's integrity or trustworthiness.

The need to view yourself and others in a particular way is especially important in relation to your attachment style because this is a fundamental way in which you interact with the world. Your brain "helps" you by providing a picture, based on your particular style, of what you expect to see in your partner and yourself. And it only takes a small amount of evidence to convince yourself that your attachment-related preconceptions are accurate, whether or not they are truly accurate or adaptive.

For example, consider Jenny, who has a preoccupied style of attachment. She feels inadequate, so she *expects* that her boyfriends will grow tired of her and then cheat. Even with her current boyfriend, Brian, who frequently expresses his love and often tries to reassure her of his commitment, she cannot give up her powerful need to protect herself from any possible abandonment. So when he showed up late for a date, she immediately interpreted this as a sign that he was probably hiding something—most likely a relationship with another woman. To her, this was also evidence that she was flawed and unlovable.

Psychologists use the term *confirmation bias* to describe the tendency of people to find ways to confirm their own beliefs. When people use this bias to confirm what they already believe about themselves (good or bad), psychologists call it *self-verification verification* (Swann, Stein-Seroussi, and Giesler, 1992). These processes operate mostly outside of awareness, so people can't see how their beliefs cause them distress. It's these unseen biased perceptions that cause people to repeat old patterns even when those patterns continually lead to pain and failure.

However, people sometimes become so unhappy with their lives or relationships that they begin to question their biases—opening up the possibility for change. For instance, Jenny had cried over many unsuccessful relationships, never understanding what went wrong. But she sensed that Brian really was a "keeper," so she did some honest soul-searching. She admitted to herself that her fears of Brian leaving her did not make sense given his consistent caring and faithfulness, and she began to question and challenge those fears. Though it didn't come naturally and took some conscious effort on her part, this led to Jenny being more and more open to trusting Brian and eventually to feeling she was lovable—after all, if *someone* could love her, then she must be worthy of love. For people who experience attachment-related anxiety, opening up to the possibility that they are worthy of love is especially important.

Challenging your tendency to self-verify and view your life with a confirmation bias is difficult, to say the least. However, you can start the process by learning what to look for in yourself.

Learning to See Yourself in a Positive Light

It's natural to think that you can change your style of interacting by just being on the lookout for when you self-verify or operate from a confirmation bias—for instance, by noting when you are unnecessarily self-critical or recognizing when you unrealistically fear rejection. While there is some truth to this, it's important to understand that such observations can be unsettling, or worse. You're likely to feel anxious, resist thinking about your observations, or just have a sense of something not being right. You are also likely to question these new, more positive observations rather than question your established biases. The reason is that they offer a perspective that challenges the very foundation of how you make sense of yourself and your relationship. As a result, they also upset your sense of comfort and safety in the world.

However, the more you can recognize your biases, the more you'll begin to be more open to—and even search out—a more objective perspective. Slowly you will begin to see yourself and your partner differently.

Confirming the "You" You Know

As mentioned earlier, people are especially motivated to verify their self-perceptions of being worthy or unworthy of love. They self-verify by selectively paying attention to, selectively remembering, and selectively interpreting information (Swann, Rentfrow, and Guinn, 2003). Note how these three principles overlap, and all lead to the same result:

Selective attention: People pay more attention to, and spend more time considering, feedback that confirms their sense of their own lovability or unlovability than feedback that disconfirms it.

Selective memory: People tend to remember feedback that confirms their sense of being worthy or unworthy of love. Sometimes they don't even process information that conflicts with their preconception, let alone remember it over time.

Selective interpretation: People tend to unquestioningly believe feedback that confirms their sense of being lovable or unlovable. They think any feedback that conflicts with their preconception is due to a mistake or deception. They also interpret absent or ambiguous evidence as support for their self-perceptions.

As a person who struggles with attachment-related anxiety, you might notice that you selectively confirm that you are not worthy of love in the following way: You attend particularly closely to any evidence that you are needy, weak, or flawed in some way; and you downplay or fail to notice your strengths or positive attributes. Then you remember things your partner has said or done that seem to confirm that you are inadequate or flawed in some essential way, or that he is likely to reject or leave you. Meanwhile, you fail to remember the times that your partner told you how wonderful you are or stood by you through a tough time. If you aren't in a relationship, you are likely to remember all the times you've been rejected, but fail to think about your lack of interest in others who have been interested in you, or about the relationships you have enjoyed even though they ultimately didn't work out.

It can be difficult to gain enough perspective to see these biases and their effects on your daily interactions. So if you need to, spend some time reviewing and applying this section, along with the following exercise, to your life.

Exercise: Observe How You Self-Verify

Review the assessment of your level of attachment-related anxiety in the section "The Basics of How You Connect" in chapter 1. This will show your sense of your worthiness of love.

Answer the following questions to help you better understand how you *maintain* your self-perception of being unworthy of love (to the extent that you do feel this way). It's an important step toward breaking the cycle. Complete it in relation to your partner, as well as to other close people in your life. Repeat the exercise daily until you have a natural awareness of these issues as you go through your days. Because the drive to self-verify can make this difficult to do, write out your answers as a way to stay focused and guide yourself. Hold on to them to help complete an exercise in the next chapter. You might also find it helpful to talk about this with a supportive partner or another person you trust.

Challenging Selective Attention

- What occurred during the day that showed you that you are worthy of love, or that at least brings into question your self-perception of being unlovable? Pick one or two situations (for instance, your partner wanted to watch TV together, or a friend phoned you).

- How did you feel in these situations? (For instance, happy, uncomfortable, confused, nothing.)

- How did you think about these situations? For instance, did you dismiss or minimize this feedback? Did you doubt the honesty or competence of the person giving it? (For example, did you assume your partner wanted to watch TV with you only out of habit?)

- Can you see how you are—or might be—self-verifying with selective attention?

Challenging Selective Memory

- What good or positive things did you do today? (Everything counts; nothing is too insignificant.)

- In what ways have family, friends, or even acquaintances shown that they appreciate you?

- In what ways did your partner show that he or she cares about you?

Challenging Selective Interpretation

- If you think someone has shown you in some way that you are unlovable, could you be misinterpreting the other person's motivation or intentions? (For example, did you misperceive his tiredness as your being uninteresting or unlovable?)

- Could you be making the feedback worse than was intended? (For instance, thinking you're flawed and unlovable when your partner was just trying to talk about something that upset him.)

- Are you downplaying your strengths and focusing on ways that you don't live up to your own unrealistic expectations or to the achievements of your partner and others?

Consider your responses in each of the sections above on challenging selective attention, memory, and interpretation. Note how you self-verify in each of these ways. What themes do you see? For instance, you might become easily jealous; or constantly be preparing to be rejected; or frequently point out to yourself that you are inadequate, flawed, or not as good as your partner. You might also struggle with thinking your partner will stop loving you once he sees the "real" you. Or you might feel upset by your partner seeming to not really care about you. Write down in detail the theme(s) that you play out, and hold on to this to use in the exercise "Revealing Your Invisible Known" in the next chapter.

♡

Confirming How You See Others

Just as people unconsciously use confirmation bias to self-verify how worthy or unworthy they feel, they also use it to maintain their sense of how emotionally available or unavailable their partners (as well as others) are.

Clearly, people who are preconditioned to think that others won't be there for them will tend to see their partners as emotionally unavailable. So they see themselves as essentially alone, and they protect themselves by being self-reliant. What's less obvious—and seemingly paradoxical—is that you can similarly experience yourself as alone when you believe that others *are* generally emotionally available. This is likely to happen when you have doubts about whether you are worthy of love, leaving you to think that those available others ultimately will reject *you*. So although you might think positively of your partner at the beginning of your relationship, these perceptions will probably turn negative over time, as you find ways to confirm that he really isn't there for you after all.

Because of your preconceptions about your partner's unavailability to you, you are likely to think that a problematic behavior on your partner's part is due to a personality trait that won't change, rather than the influence of a situation or context. For instance, if your partner doesn't call from his job one day, you might jump to the conclusion that it's due to a lack of caring, or even to a more malicious intent of playing with your emotions—as opposed to the possibility that he was particularly busy at work. The more anxiously attached you are, the more likely this will happen when you are in a bad mood. This will happen less when you are feeling good or are basically happy in your relationship. By contrast, if you have a highly avoidant partner, he will think this way even when he is feeling emotionally stable and your relationship is going well.

The bias toward seeing others as emotionally unavailable creates "blind spots." You simply don't "see" how you maintain your belief that your partner is unavailable. Just as with self-verification, your bias does this through selective attention, selective memory, and selective interpretation—but this time, it's more about the other person.

Closed-Loop Relationships

Every time Dick sees Jane around the house, he ridicules her.
Every time Jane sees Dick, she tries to avoid him.
Dick stokes his feelings of superiority by ridiculing Jane.
Jane's avoidance reinforces Dick's feelings of superiority.

Every time Jane sees Dick, she tries to avoid him.
Every time Dick sees Jane, he ridicules her.
Jane stokes her feelings of inferiority by avoiding Dick.
Dick's ridicule reinforces Jane's feelings of inferiority.

Partners maintain a balance between them that they both resist changing, even when the relationship is strained. Each person reinforces his or her own self-view by behaving in a way consistent with it. This behavior also elicits responses from the other partner that confirm this self-perception. With such feedback "proving" what they already "know" about themselves, people again act in line with their self-perceptions…it's a closed loop.

In a bizarre way, the above pattern of interaction gives both Dick *and* Jane a sense of safety—they know what to expect from themselves and each other, and how to respond. This predictability provides a comfort even for Jane—how much harder would it be for her if Dick was sometimes really nice and other times nasty? And imagine how confusing and uncomfortable it would be for Jane—even if it also felt good—if Dick treated her consistently well when she deeply believed that she was unlovable and expected him to reject her at any moment.

When others treat you in a way that fits with your self-perceptions, you feel validated and the relationship feels comfortably familiar, even if it is painful. You are also more likely to continue the relationship than if the person did not seem to really "get" you. For example, as you might assume, secure people who feel good about themselves want to be around others who think highly of them. However—and this is perhaps not as intuitive—anxious people with low self-esteem often leave when their partners persist in viewing them as precious and lovable. Instead, they tend to stay with and marry less supportive partners—which, of course, just reinforces their sense of being unlovable. This places them in a situation where there is legal and social pressure to stay in a relationship that is unhealthy for them.

Because such predictability is comforting, any changes in a relationship—even *positive* ones—are often met with resistance. People feel pulled by themselves, as well as by their partners and others, to return to more predictable ways. Although this draw to old patterns is strong, people *can* develop new ones. When a person does change, some old relationships accommodate to the change, others die off, and new relationships develop from the "new self." Recognizing and accepting this ahead of time can ease the transition.

A good example of this was provided in the movie *Pretty Woman* (1990). I'm not talking about the title character, but about Edward (Richard Gere), a strong, capable, and extremely successful businessman whose approach to life is coldly calculating. When he meets a call girl, Vivian (Julia Roberts), she challenges him to open up. He resists at first, preferring to hold on to his more distant persona. But with time and the new emotionally intimate relationship, he becomes a warmer person. Then he begins to approach his work more humanely. These changes wreak havoc. His lawyer rails against this change, and the other "suits" who work for him balk. But in grand Hollywood style, the audience is left to believe that Edward is a changed man. He marries the woman who has changed him, and his employees must learn to adjust to the new him or find a new job.

Pursuit-Withdrawal: A Common Relationship Problem

One of the most common problematic relationship styles is the pursuit-withdrawal pattern, which emerges between an anxiously attached partner (more frequently a woman) and an avoidant partner. In fact, it's so common that there's a good chance that you've experienced it at some point. It works like this: Each time the anxious partner steps forward or leans in for closeness, the avoidant partner pulls back, which prompts the anxious partner to try to get close again. Sometimes it can be hard to see this dance of intimacy beneath everyday topics, discussions, and interactions. To get a sense of how this plays out, consider Lucy and Ken. After dating for about a year, they moved in together. Unfortunately, within just a few months, their relationship had become increasingly strained:

Lucy: When you come home, you barely even say hi to me.

Ken: Well, I'm tired and need a chance to just breathe. But after I've settled in, I do ask you about your day, and you give me the cold shoulder.

Lucy: Sure, you come down after having showered, changed clothes, and relaxed a while. Meanwhile, I'm stressing out getting dinner on the table for us. You never even offer to help. I get home from work not that long before you, so I'm tired, too.

Ken: (*weakly*) I've tried to help, but you don't even like how I set the table.

Lucy: You call what you do setting the table? Dropping a napkin and fork near our chairs hardly qualifies. I have to go back and fold the napkin and put the fork on it. You do everything like that—halfway—and then I have to finish it up.

Ken: (*shrugs his shoulders*) No matter what I do, you're not happy.

Lucy: I just wish you would do some things around the house unprompted by me; and *finish* what you start. How hard is that? But you don't, and I end up having to do everything by myself—like the laundry and cleaning up and even planning our vacations. You say you love me, but I don't feel it anymore. I just feel so alone in it all.

Ken: (*matter-of-fact manner*) Well, I promise to do a better job setting the table; and I'll do more laundry, too.

Doesn't sound very promising, does it? Interestingly, they both *think* they're working on the relationship, but...

Like Lucy, you might get caught in this pattern, focusing on either wanting to feel connected or on feeling a lack of connection; sometimes both. And so you protest against your partner's distance. Lucy does this by demanding attention and responsiveness. But her avoidant partner's distance reinforces her sense of not being loved and her fear that she is not worthy of love. Desperate, she does all she can to fight for her relationship, including making many concessions to her partner, but also making frantic demands for more responsiveness from him. Their interactions make her feel lonely and reinforce her negative thinking about him and their relationship (for examples, see the table that follows). Steeped in her own emotions, she does not recognize his distress in response to her demands.

Or maybe you're more like Ken. You might be a generally avoidant person, but feel anxiety as well. An avoidant person caught in this pattern focuses on wanting to keep an emotionally safe distance and to stonewall his partner's anger or disapproval. Ken is more comfortable when he is independent and in a powerful—not vulnerable—position with Lucy. When she becomes upset, he tries to emotionally distance himself from her feelings and from his own fears of separation. He does this by thinking about her in a negative way (for examples, see the table). He also withdraws, turning more strongly to his inclination to be self-reliant. In doing this, he fails to recognize or understand Lucy's bids for closeness, warmth, and reassurance; or how his lack of emotional expressiveness and lack of warmth make her feel painfully alone.

COMMON THOUGHTS IN PURSUIT-WITHDRAWAL DYNAMIC	
Anxiously attached partner focuses on wanting more connection:	Avoidantly attached partner focuses on wanting a safe distance from her partner's anger or disapproval:
I'm not a priority. I have to take care of everything. If only I was smarter/more attractive, he'd be more interested in me. We don't do anything together. He doesn't care how I feel. He's never around. He never even gives me a card for my birthday. He doesn't care what I think. He isn't affectionate at all—there's no romance or passion in our relationship. He's going to leave.	I just try to do what she wants so she won't get angry. I never do anything right in her eyes. I can never make her happy. I don't know what to do to make her happy. She's never interested in sex. She's too needy. She's too emotional. She has so much baggage. She's always upset about something. I'd be better off alone.
Note: Women are more often anxiously attached and men are more often avoidant in these situations. However, there are many couples with the opposite pattern.	

The most frequent long-term pattern for these couples is that both partners become more extreme in their positions. However, for many of them, there is eventually a flip in their roles. Over years, the avoidant person becomes more distant and hostile; and the anxious person becomes more upset and resorts to more intense protest behaviors, such as also being hostile or threatening to leave. But in between stormy times, the anxious person reflects on positive memories and feelings, leading her to reach out in a more positive, reconciliatory way. The avoidant partner, however, remains withdrawn and angry. Gradually, the anxious partner gives up trying. Often, in those couples that marry, the wife—who is likely the anxious partner—decides to leave after the children grow up and move out (though she doesn't always wait that long). Taken unawares, the husband then sometimes desperately pursues her. Although complex, this is a very common scenario.

The pursuit-withdrawal dynamic goes especially wrong in some relationships, which end up being controlling and sometimes abusive. An anxious partner may resort to intimidation or aggression in order to get attention, reassurance, or love from an unresponsive and detached partner. Occasionally, it's the avoidant partner who is aggressive, though this is more often passive aggression—expressed, for instance, in cold silence, rolling eyes, or other ways of being disrespectful. This behavior is the avoidant partner's way of trying to get the anxious partner to back off.

Exercise: What Would a Fly on the Wall See in Your Home?

It can be very enlightening to pay attention to the patterns of communication in your relationship—especially those related to conflicts. Noting the feelings, thoughts, and actions of each partner can help to provide important insights. Consider the following example:

Jill *feels* hurt that Paul doesn't spend time with her on the weekends and instead hangs out with his friends. She *thinks* he doesn't care. She expresses this by crying and telling him he's selfish. Paul *feels* attacked, *thinks* she is overreacting, and *reacts* by withdrawing. Jill *feels* hurt, and the cycle repeats.

With this in mind, think of a conflict that tends to repeat in your relationship. Now consider the following questions related to it. (Although these questions assume that you are the one initially upset, you can modify them to accommodate your partner initiating the conflict.)

As the conflict is going on…

FEELING: How are you feeling about what's happening?

THOUGHT: What are you thinking about your partner?

ACTION: How do you express the problem?

FEELING: What do you imagine your partner is feeling on the receiving end?

THOUGHT: What do you imagine your partner is thinking about you?

ACTION: How does your partner respond?

Note how the interaction continues and how it finally ends (for instance, there is an explosion; or both of you withdraw). For the questions about your partner's experience, it can be helpful to ask your partner what he was feeling and thinking—but only if you can talk about this productively with him. Otherwise, try empathizing with him to imagine his responses; or ask someone you trust for help.

Review Your Patterns

- How do you and your partner affect each other's feelings and actions?

- What patterns do you notice?

- How does this interaction reinforce your beliefs about how worthy of love you are?

- How does this interaction reinforce your beliefs about how emotionally available your partner is?

At an appropriate, calm time, you might want to talk with your partner about this exercise, sharing the insights it's given you. You might also ask your partner about how the interactions affect his sense of being worthy of love and his sense of how emotionally available you are.

There is a lot here to make sense of within yourself, as well as to try to work through with your partner. So this is an area that you might find helpful to spend some time reviewing. You might also find it helpful to think this through a bit now, then return to it again at a later time.

♡

Summary: Gaining Perspective

In this chapter, I have shown how your attachment style, self-verification, and the confirmation bias combine to keep you repeating old patterns. They distort your perceptions and support frequently counterproductive ways of viewing yourself and your partners (past, present, and future). That's a lot to try to understand and really absorb. To fully get it, you need to spend some time turning it over in your mind. And you absolutely need to apply it to how you've lived your life, and continue to do so.

In the next chapter, I lay out more of the nitty-gritty about how it's possible to know all of this information in an abstract and still be blind to your problematic ways of interacting in the world. This understanding can help open your eyes to ways you can break the pattern and establish happier, healthier relationships.

Chapter 4

Overcoming Obstacles

Even when people are aware of their relationship patterns and are motivated to change, they often unconsciously undermine their attempts at self-improvement. For instance, Vito loved Miranda and knew that his intense (and unjustified) jealousy upset her. He worried that he would drive her away, so he committed himself to placing trust in her, especially after she yelled at him for snooping on her cell phone. One week later, though, he impulsively picked up Miranda's phone to see if she had been texting other men. With her just in the next room, this behavior appeared blatantly self-destructive, but that was certainly not the intent. This happened only one day after he saw a former girlfriend happily holding the hand of a man at the mall. Though misguided and risky, his quick peek at Miranda's phone was actually his attempt to *help* himself regain his sense of security.

As I've noted, people need a sense of security to function in daily life. The drive to find it is especially heightened when you are scared of losing your partner. This can trigger you to reexperience the same primal panic you might have felt as an infant, when every danger threatened your survival and you desperately searched for your parents to comfort and protect you. In other words, when you sense that your partner might not be there for you, you can feel—at a core level— *scared to death*. Or when you try to change in ways that conflict with your attachment style, which is designed to keep you safe, you are likely to instinctively return to your familiar attachment behaviors— even if those behaviors (like Vito's) are counterproductive and fly in the face of your conscious commitment to "do better." This way of understanding behavior is not always intuitive and can be confusing. So let's take a closer look.

Self-Deception

People's attachment styles and attachment-related behaviors are so much a part of who they are—and can be so strongly motivated by primal panic—that it is extremely difficult for them to recognize all the ways in which they self-verify, even when they know to look for this bias. Sometimes their bias can be so all-encompassing that it prevents awareness of problems even when they become glaring.

For instance, some anxiously attached people turn to alcohol as a way to soothe their distress after feeling rejected. Even when this unhealthy coping crosses the line into alcoholism, they often don't realize or acknowledge the full extent of their problem because that would only upset them more. Sometimes they remain in denial even after repeatedly being caught driving drunk. Similarly, many anxiously attached women blame themselves when they are verbally abused and beaten by a partner—something that happens all too often—and so they choose to stay in that relationship. For those on the outside looking in, it can be incomprehensible how those suffering can't clearly see the problems and solutions (for instance, *Just stop drinking*, or *Leave the bastard*).

Even more maddening to onlookers is the on-again-off-again acknowledgment of problems. For instance, consider Linda. She thought she had "everything"—loving husband, wonderful kids, no financial worries—but she was depressed. She was also angry with herself because she didn't think she had any right to be unhappy. Yet even in our first session it was clear that she felt her husband didn't respect her, and that she'd devoted her life to him (and others) so much that she didn't do anything for herself—and so she felt deprived. When I repeated her words to that effect, she responded as if she was hearing it for the first time. "I just said that, didn't I? Wow." But only a few minutes later, she was again lamenting that she didn't know why she was so unhappy.

She clearly did know on some level that these struggles existed, or she couldn't have told me about them. But she also couldn't let them reside fully and comfortably in her consciousness. So, in a sense, she knew them but didn't know them. You experience this when you sense that something conflicts with your attachment style or challenges established patterns of your identity, yet don't fully acknowledge it. It's a protective way of distancing you from a psychological threat or emotional pain (a dynamic often referred to by therapists as "dissociation"). You can also get a sense of "knowing-but-not-knowing" in this way: Consider someone who received attention as an infant only when she became highly emotional. Based on this early experience, she might continue a pattern of being overly emotional with others well into adulthood. Although she's aware of being an emotional person, she does not consciously know that's her way of getting close to others—which contrasts with Linda's partial awareness of why she was unhappy. I call both of these knowing-but-not-knowing experiences the *invisible known.*

(I have adapted this term from British psychoanalyst Christopher Bollas [1987], who introduced the term *unthought known* to specifically describe those experiences that people can't remember because they originate prior to about age three.)

When you struggle with understanding why it's so hard to change the ways you act in relationships, consider thinking about your past as a way to tap into the invisible known. Because patterns are established based on previous experiences (with childhood often having a strong influence), people sometimes respond to present situations in a way that only makes sense when one considers their past. In the case of Linda, she spent her childhood trying unsuccessfully to please her mother, who treated her harshly. With this information, it was not hard to understand how she developed a style of being extra nice to people and working hard to avoid their wrath. While her "niceness" helped her to make many friends, it also frequently left her feeling unimportant. Not surprisingly, she struggled with the invisible known and was unable to talk honestly to her husband about many concerns between them—concerns that piled up over the years. Eventually she became distressed enough to seek therapy.

Unfortunately, when you have unhealthy ways of coping or relating to others, your attempts to fix problems and cope often become a vicious cycle. They make things worse—and perpetuate the closed-loop patterns discussed in the last chapter. Linda's situation is a good example of this. She responded to her fear of rejection by being extra nice, but this led to her feeling unimportant and rejected, which she responded to by trying even harder to be nice. Similarly, the problem drinker uses alcohol to calm his distress, which leads to more problems and more distress. He responds by again trying to numb himself with alcohol, thus starting the pattern over again—even as his marriage falls apart and his ability to function at work deteriorates. And as any excessively perfectionistic person will tell you, the harder he tries to get everything right, the more problems he sees with his performance.

The Logic Stops Here

You might wonder, "Okay, I get the whole *invisible known* idea, but why can't people just change once these experiences are pointed out?"

This seems logical—like being able to open a safe once you're given the combination. But it's not that easy. The very complexity that enables you to develop your identity, so that you can function relatively easily in your life, also frequently makes such simple solutions ineffective. People often have conflicting thoughts or beliefs, or get feedback that clashes with their beliefs; and such conflicts cause inner tension that psychologists call *cognitive dissonance*. It's an extremely uncomfortable experience that people unconsciously go to great lengths to avoid. In their book *Mistakes Were Made*, psychologists Carol Tavris and Elliot Aronson explain, "In a sense, dissonance theory is a theory of blind spots—of how and why people unintentionally blind themselves so that they fail to notice vital events and information that might throw them into dissonance, making them question their behavior or their convictions" (2007, 42).

To understand how this affects your attachment style and relationships, remember that you establish your attachment style to feel safe and secure in the world. This way of being begins to form in childhood and is strengthened through daily experiences over a lifetime of self-verification and confirmation bias—your attempt to *prove* that you are who you think you are (for instance, unworthy of love) and that others are who you think they are (for instance, available attachment figures).

To clarify, consider an anxiously attached woman with low self-esteem. She might momentarily feel good about her boyfriend complimenting her, but this will create cognitive dissonance. So she will quickly revert to viewing herself negatively, complete with an assortment of reasons to rationalize why she's "undeserving"—all of which resolves her dissonance by self-verifying (and reinforcing) her negative self-image. This is how cognitive dissonance and self-verification work together to block change.

To complicate matters, how people feel about past events can keep them from letting go of those events and cause them to act in unhealthy ways or to struggle with certain situations. For instance, the fact that a woman intellectually knows that she was sexually abused as a child does not magically relieve her of the emotional pain from those experiences, any more than knowing that someone hit you over the head with a brick can heal your fractured skull. So she might try to avoid thinking about those experiences even as she continues to feel uncomfortable with physical intimacy. In situations like this, when people are compelled to avoid emotional pain or the reasons for it, they are left to exist with the invisible known—which has its own nagging pain—and to blindly repeat problematic behaviors or experiences.

While it might seem to make sense to advise yourself to "just let it go; it's in the past," this advice is useless—or worse. No one *wants* to feel upset; believing that you are purposely torturing yourself only adds to your pain.

Even people who are characteristically avoidant and relatively good at denying emotional pain still have to contend with the invisible known when it becomes so painful or destructive that they are forced to face it. For instance, Laura was a stay-at-home mother who used self-discipline to maintain structure for herself and to help her to impose structure on her family. However, as her children grew older, they began to challenge her control and she began to lose her temper. Their emerging independence unleashed her emotions (which she had always done her best to suppress) and her self-doubts (which she had rarely even acknowledged to herself). Her distress made it impossible for her to remain comfortably self-reliant and revealed just how alone she had felt in her marriage. Somewhere deep inside, she had always known that she felt distant from her husband—and that she, in part, created this divide.

The now-you-see-it-now-you-don't quality of the invisible known makes confronting it difficult. To fully acknowledge and question it, people must persistently challenge the rules that they *implicitly* live by, such as expecting that others won't truly love them and be there for them. For instance, Laura was able—over the course of therapy—to acknowledge that she never fully trusted her husband to be support-ive, so she had usually dismissed his caring gestures and thought more about how he let her down. As she risked being vulnerable by sharing this with her husband, she found that he was understanding and also wanted a closer relationship. By opening up to experiencing yourself and others differently, you can begin to loosen your firm grip on the past and heal from old hurts. This can help you change how you relate to yourself and others in the present.

Exercise: Revealing Your Invisible Known

In the last chapter, you completed the "Observe How You Self-Verify" exercise, which helped you to identify ways in which you self-verify. Review your answers or complete the exercise again.

Now, for this chapter's exercise, we'll take it a step further.

Make note of a theme or two that you chose to focus on. Read the themes that you identified when completing that exercise in the last chapter. Then reconnect with your observations of how you self-verified to play them out.

Ask yourself:

- How did you feel as you challenged your selective attention, selective memory, and selective interpretation (for instance, tension, discomfort)?

- How did your bias affect your beliefs about yourself?

Revealing your invisible known. You might find that you can see your bias, but then lose your awareness of it as you get sucked into the bias itself. For example, you might see that you tend to dismiss your partner's true caring as his just meeting an obligation. But rather than allow yourself to recognize that your bias keeps you from being open to the possibility of his love, you might get caught up in proving to yourself that he doesn't really love you and that he might leave at any time. Seeing your bias and then having it disappear is evidence of the invisible known. It's just like a magic trick—now you see it, now you don't!

Practice this exercise again and again with different examples of the same themes. Repeating it will help you become increasingly aware of how your invisible known directs your feelings and behaviors. It will also help you to see your part in your relationship problems.

It can be very helpful and enlightening to share your observations, thoughts, and feelings with someone supportive in your life—maybe even your partner. Journaling about them can also help.

♡

How Pain Motivates Change

When people with an anxious attachment style overperform in an effort to prove their value, they are often simultaneously trying to hide their fear of rejection, their sense of feeling flawed, and other struggles related to themselves and others. Each time these problems recur, they are unconsciously shoved into the proverbial closet, away from awareness (as mentioned earlier, many therapists refer to this as *dissociation*). Eventually the "junk" (and problems related to it) pushes to come out—much like the popular cartoon of a bulging door of an overstuffed closet. People react to their growing distress in many ways, such as experiencing depression, anxiety, insomnia, general fatigue, or chronic back pain. They might also overeat, abuse alcohol, or shop to excess.

Even when you can recognize intellectually that a particular bias causes you distress, you may not pay much actual attention to it.

Instead, you experience a sense of knowing that it is "just the way things are." You might "know" that you are unlovable, and you might also "know" that others won't reliably be there for you. As Robert Burton (2008) effectively argued in his book *On Being Certain: Believing You Are Right Even When You're Not*, people's sense of knowing is beyond their control and cannot be easily argued away. It's a powerful pull for them to remain as they've always been, even when they are engaging in self-defeating behaviors.

For instance, highly anxiously attached people with low self-esteem can listen to advice on how to build themselves up; they can think positive thoughts; they can invest themselves in a multitude of ways to feel good—but often all to no avail. On a deep level, they "know" that they are unacceptable in some essential way. Remember, they developed their identity over time, and it provides them with a sense of safety. But eventually many of them feel so much distress that they are forced to consider that something must change—even if they don't know what it is.

Even avoidant people, who tend to maintain an in-control manner, are sometimes pushed out of their comfort zone by severe and chronic stressors. The feelings of being alone and vulnerable that they have defended against their whole lives fail them, and so they are forced to attend to emotional pain. At these times, they are sometimes willing—if not exactly eager—to try something different.

So whatever your attachment style, you are likely to challenge the status quo only after feeling significant distress or emotional pain. By taking the risk of really seeing and challenging current biases of yourself and others, you become free to consider new perspectives—a difficult feat given that the purpose of your attachment style is to keep you feeling safe and sound in the world. One of my patients shared an insightful quote to explain why she finally came to therapy after years of struggling with this conflict: "And the day came when the risk to remain tight in the bud was more painful than the risk it took to blossom." (The source of this quotation is unknown, though it has sometimes been attributed to Anaïs Nin.)

The Need for New Experiences

Feeling emotional pain and understanding how you maintain problematic patterns do not tell you how to be different or automatically establish healthier patterns. This has to develop over time with new experiences. For example, you might realize that you tend to be guarded with everyone in your current life, even your spouse, because you felt criticized or emotionally abandoned as a child by your parents; or because a former fiancé cheated on you with your closest friend. However, even after you realize this, you still have a few tasks ahead of you if you want to change. You must allow yourself to let down your defenses and experience vulnerability within a caring relationship. Then you'll need to develop the inner resilience to continue reaching out even after you feel hurt by your new love (which *will* happen eventually in any close relationship). But there's no need to stress too much about this. Just proceed slowly. You'll want to feel yourself stretch, but not so much that you snap.

To illustrate further, consider Jessie. Her parents loved her, but they were by nature somewhat emotionally distant. They could smile and laugh and have a "normal" family life, but they tended to focus on their children's achievements rather than on relating to their children's more personal qualities and experiences. When Jessie and her siblings were sad or hurt or distressed in any way, her parents responded with directives not to whine and with a pull-yourself-up-by-the-bootstraps mentality.

Jessie learned not to complain. She came to believe that her imperfect performance and distressing feelings not only meant that she wouldn't be loved, but also that she was essentially flawed and unworthy of love. No matter what accomplishments she achieved in life (and there were many), she never felt good enough. She was always waiting for others to see her mistakes and recognize her unworthiness— and reject her. Unfortunately, this also meant that she didn't trust any man who showed interest in her unless he was also rejecting in some way. As you might imagine, the relationships she had with men were brief and emotionally painful.

For Jessie, like many people who are raised in families that make acceptance contingent on performance, being self-critical was a way of coping that made sense—she was trying to fix all the problems in her performance so that her parents would be proud of her and love her. As an adult, her "overlearned" self-criticism was a part of her identity that she used to try to help herself in three important ways. First, by narrowly focusing on how she could improve her performance, she could sometimes avoid the intolerable distress of knowing she was less than perfect and unlovable. Second, she was more directly trying to ward off rejection, which she thought would happen if she failed in any way. And last but not least, her extra efforts frequently paid off in others' being happy with her performance (not that she could allow herself to fully take this in).

When Jessie began therapy, she was desperate to be free from her self-attacks, but she couldn't figure out how to escape. She was all too aware that the *desire* for a healthier, happier way of being does not in itself reveal a map for how to get there. To leave behind those old, beaten-down, and circular paths, you must devise an effective escape route (or be helped by someone who has such a plan). For Jessie, that route was learning to value her whole self, not just what she could accomplish. Once she succeeded in doing this, she was able to leave her critical self behind, and free to enjoy her life and relationships. Of course, as with so much in life, "the devil is in the details." The next chapter will offer some essential guidelines on how you can develop a personalized escape route.

PART THREE

Compassionate Self-Awareness: The Antidote to Relationship Anxiety

Chapter 5

A Path to Deep,
Lasting Security

By this point in the book, you know your attachment style. You understand what causes you to perpetuate unhealthy and ineffective ways of seeing yourself and your partner. These are extremely important insights. But as you increase your self-awareness, you will also feel a strong pull to self-verify your old perceptions of yourself. You'll find ways to continue seeing yourself, your partner, and your relationship as you always have, and to resist the potentially healing influence of what you are learning about yourself. If you persist, though, a new perspective will prevail. You will be freer to learn how to nurture a happier relationship, and maybe even change your attachment style. While this offers great hope, the billion-dollar question is *how to do it*—how can you maintain insight into unhealthy patterns and actually (finally) nurture a happy relationship?

When faced with this question, it's natural for people to look for direct answers—a list of fail-safe strategies or tactics for meeting these challenges. They look for concrete tools: *Do this. Don't do that.* Often, however, the direct methods alone fail. People can't effectively use the "good" advice they are given because their inner environment supports the unhealthy status quo.

What's needed is a way to change that core environment—a way that directly improves how you relate to yourself and emotionally connect with your partner. This makes me think about what happened with a small plant I once had. Its green leaves gave my office a little warmth, despite its lack of flowers. But when I moved to an office with a large wall of windows that faced the morning sun, pink blooms exploded all over it and brightened up my office, as well as my mood. Similarly, people can get the "sunshine" they need to blossom from loving relationships.

If you are always standing in the shadows of your attachment-related anxiety, there are two ways you can find happiness in your relationships—and even "earn" secure attachment—which I touched on in chapter 2. One way is with an emotionally available attachment figure who is loving, accepting, and consistently available. This could be a romantic partner, but not necessarily. This figure could also be a family member, a friend, a clergyperson, a therapist, a mentor, or even God. Really, it can be anyone whom you feel that you can turn to for support.

The other way is through what I call *compassionate self-awareness*—an awareness of yourself from the perspective of having a concern for, and a desire to lessen, your own suffering. In both cases, love seeps in over time to comfort and reassure you that you are worthy of it. Ultimately, to earn secure attachment, you must be open to love from an emotionally available attachment figure *and* be open to being compassionately self-aware.

Fortunately, a truly loving partner can help you develop compassionate self-awareness; and compassionate self-awareness can help you be more open to a truly loving partner. Each of these can build on the other—a little bit at a time—to help you feel more worthy of love, see your partner in a more positive light, and work with your partner to nurture a happy, healthy relationship. In addition, they can help you to create a sense (or, more accurately, a mental representation) of your partner—and ultimately yourself—that you can carry with you wherever you go, which can comfort and reassure you in times of distress.

The idea that having the right partner can help you to feel loved and happy is what dreams—and romantic stories—are made of. You can intuitively understand it. But compassionate self-awareness needs some explaining. The concept grew out of my gnawing curiosity about what various areas of psychological literature (not just the ones that I knew of) had to say about creating personal change. As I plowed through piles of research and reflected on my clinical experience, the idea of compassionate self-awareness presented itself as vitally important in personal change and healing. Its two main elements are *self-awareness* and *self-compassion*, both of which I will explain in depth below. Then, in the following chapters, I will provide you with detailed exercises for developing the different parts of this essential skill set.

Self-Awareness

To improve your intimate relationships, you must look at your role in creating problems—or at what you do to prevent relationships from even getting started. Yet, as I've explained, people's biases tend to blind them to these insights. So developing self-awareness and making effective use of it can be tricky.

But if you persist in observing your tendency to confirm your pre-conceptions of yourself and your partner (or potential partner), you will begin to see these biases more easily and more clearly. No longer mistaking perceptions as absolute truth, you will be freer to initiate positive changes.

It's helpful to think of self-awareness as comprised of awareness of emotions, awareness of thoughts, and *mentalizing*—all of which I will describe below.

Awareness of Emotions

Emotions provide a richness of experience that would be lacking in a purely intellectual existence. It's the difference, for instance, between *knowing* a new romantic interest is a good fit for you on paper and actually *feeling* on cloud nine.

By opening up to emotions, people can sometimes identify beliefs or experiences that they were previously unaware of, or that they did not realize the strength of. For instance, a woman might realize she is in love with a friend only after feeling pangs of jealousy about his dating someone else. Another example is a woman who knows she likes spending time alone, but only realizes just how important this is when her new boyfriend becomes clingy. Emotions not only breathe life into existence; they also provide information for us to act on.

Along with being in touch with their emotions, people need to be able to *self-regulate*—or manage—them so that they don't get over-whelmed. They try to do this in a number of different ways, many of which fail—and some of which you might relate to. For instance, they might try to suppress, deny, or numb distressing feelings. But when those tactics are used too often, the feelings are likely to go underground, only to come back out at a later time—and with a vengeance, often leaving people anxious, depressed, or angry. A different approach is when people ruminate, repeatedly reviewing the causes and consequences of a problem as they look for a solution. But when the problem has no real or clear answer, they remain caught in a cycle of feeling upset and anxious, trying to problem solve to reduce their distress, failing to fix their problem, and then feeling more anxious. Or they become so overwhelmed that all of their emotions feel like one big boulder mounted firmly on their chest.

By contrast, people who self-regulate effectively are able to tolerate and accept their emotions. They might use the coping strategies I mentioned above, but they do it without working against themselves in other ways. For instance, they might suppress their emotions while at work, but allow themselves to get upset at home and talk about their feelings with their partners and others. Because they don't feel particularly threatened by their distress, they don't defend too strongly against it. This allows them to be more fully self-aware. As a result, they are able to ride the wave of their emotions rather than feeling like they are drowning in them.

To help clarify, consider someone who is grieving over the death of a close friend. If this person is frightened by or wants to avoid his grief, he might shut off his feelings, leaving him stuck in emotional numbness (though protected from the pain) and unable to truly connect with others in a deep way. In contrast, someone who is more accepting of grief is generally able to share it with loved ones and maintain emotionally close relationships. Although struggling with negative emotions is always painful, those who can self-regulate effectively do not feel emotional suffering (distress about their distress) as much as people who fight their emotions.

Sometimes people think that acknowledging a difficult situation means that they then need to either be resigned to it or act on it. If they are not prepared to do either, they try to deny their experience. And in the end, they remain distressed without a way to address it.

For example, Amelia doesn't want to accept that her husband is unkind to her because she fears that she would then need to either leave him, which she is not ready to do, or permanently resign herself to being unhappy. Actually, her feelings do not mean either of these things. They simply mean that she is unhappy right now. Once she acknowledges and accepts this, she will feel in sync with herself, which will give her a different perspective on her problem. She will likely develop new realizations and options—like discovering she would actually be happier without him, or that they can work on their marriage together. Of course, she can always decide to resign herself to the situation; but even then she would be doing it with a different frame of mind, which might enable her to consciously decide the best ways to continue within the marriage.

Distinguishing Thoughts and Emotions

It is important to know the difference between thoughts and feelings. You may be surprised to find out that many people confuse them. For instance, it would not be uncommon for someone to say, "I feel like I was too quiet on that date." This, of course, is a thought and not an emotion. Emotions are a combination of being aroused in a particular way and the meaning we put to that arousal. So you might *feel embarrassed* about not saying much on a date.

When people mistake their thoughts for emotions, their real emotions remain unexplored. Simply recognizing this mistake and then focusing on feelings often leads people to *experience* themselves in a more emotional way. For instance, once you realize you feel embarrassed, you might also realize you are afraid of being judged. And then you can seek reassurance or support; or you might realize that your fear is unnecessary.

To illustrate how poor emotional self-awareness can be a problem, consider a situation that frequently occurs in therapy. A woman—let's use the name Maxine—is struggling with her husband's infidelity. She says, "I feel like I can't trust him anymore. And, really, how can I? He would tell me he was at work when he was really…" And off she goes, telling me all about the awful things he has done. Her speech is rapid and she sounds angry—the more she talks, the more upset, overwhelmed, and confused she becomes. Despite being emotional, her suspicions and the examples of his dishonesty are thoughts, not feelings. So I refocus her on what she is feeling. With some prompting, she acknowledges feeling angry, betrayed, sad, scared, and hurt. She cries as she connects with all of these emotions; and she feels heard. Despite the cliché of a therapist trying to get patients to cry, my focus (and the helpful part of this interchange) is to connect her with her feelings and help her feel heard; crying is just the inevitable outcome of her doing that. Whether or not she wants to work on fixing her marriage, she is in touch with the pain that needs healing, and so she can begin to work on easing that pain.

Exercise: Opening Up to Emotion

Intertwined with naming your emotions is the *way* that you identify them. You must step out of your experiences enough to be able to make sense of them. This stepping out lessens your immersion in your emotions—even if only for a moment. To help you understand, consider how you feel right now. Really, please do that right now. I can wait a minute.

Notice how you shifted from thinking about focusing on your feelings to paying attention to your feelings to thinking about the label for them. This ability to shift attention can be very helpful in allowing you to *have* your feelings while not getting *consumed* by them—especially when they're strong feelings.

The best way to practice this is with low-intensity emotions, which have less of a chance of overwhelming you. Just as you stopped moments ago to consider your feelings, make it a practice to do this at different times during your day. For example, you can do it at mealtime, before leaving your house in the morning, or upon arriving at your office. The important point is for you to learn how to guide the way you experience your emotions—heightening your awareness of them, and moving between being *in* them and consciously *observing* them.

With practice, you will be better able to do this with more intense emotions. And the better you are at doing it, the freer you will be to view your situation with some perspective—and perhaps consider alternative ways to understand or respond to your situation.

If, like many people, you have some trouble identifying your specific emotions, don't worry. That's a common problem, and one that an exercise in the next chapter will address.

♡

Awareness of Thoughts

How you experience yourself and your beliefs about yourself is affected by your thinking. For instance, you reinforce self-doubts and low self-esteem when you repeat beliefs, such as "Danny doesn't really love me. He just stays with me because he feels sorry for me." Those thoughts also trigger emotions, such as sadness and fear of rejection.

Whether you realize it or not, you have a running subtext of thoughts throughout your day. Bringing that subtext to consciousness can be extremely helpful in learning how you perpetuate unhappiness within yourself and your relationship. With that awareness, you also have an opportunity to work on change. Sometimes even just the awareness itself is enough to facilitate change.

Exercise: Experimenting with Your Thoughts

This simple exercise is a powerful demonstration of how your thinking affects you on many levels. Find a quiet place to complete it. It will take only a few minutes.

Sit comfortably, take a deep breath or two, and close your eyes.

Slowly scan your body from your toes up to the top of your head. Be aware of any sensations, such as muscle tension, the sensation of breathing, or your heart beating.

Bring to mind a negative thought about yourself. Pick one that you tend to struggle with. Hold it in your mind and repeat it.

Pay attention to how this affects you. What sensations do you feel? How does it affect your emotions and your thoughts?

It's likely that you will feel worse when you focus on negative self-perceptions. You might notice increased tightness in your chest or churning in your stomach. You might also be aware of feeling sad or angry with yourself, or of having a cascade of other negative thoughts.

Now do this exercise again—but a little differently. Before beginning, think of a time when you felt good about yourself. What positive thoughts did you have about yourself? Use these thoughts as the focus as you complete this exercise. If you tend to be self-critical or slow to appreciate your positive qualities, you will find this more difficult to do. However, in doing it, you will notice more positive experiences (even if they're fleeting), such as more relaxed muscles, a sense of being lighter or happier, and maybe even more positive thoughts.

♡

Mentalizing

The third, and last, part of self-awareness is mentalizing, which is a process associated with psychoanalyst Peter Fonagy and his colleagues (Fonagy, Gergely, Jurist, and Target, 2002; Slade, 2008). They have explained this as a process in which people experience themselves and the world through their minds. This allows them to take a *reflective stance*—to think about the psychological reasons for their own and others' behavior. Importantly, however, mentalizing also involves being emotionally connected while having that reflective stance. Those who have a strong mentalizing ability sense that they can change the very nature of their experiences by thinking about them differently.

Implicit in mentalizing is the assumption that people have shared experiences. This *common humanity*, as described by researcher Kristin Neff (2008), naturally gives people a sense of connection and understanding for themselves and others. They can feel empathy and compassion for those in pain because they can relate. (I will discuss this in detail later in this chapter.)

Too often, however, anxiously attached people don't fully feel that they are a part of this common humanity. As a result, while they might understand why other people do and feel as they do (it's only human), they don't apply this same understanding to themselves. And though they have compassion for others, they experience themselves as flawed in a way that makes them feel undeserving of compassion—and too often inclined to fault themselves for relationship problems. Over time, though, their repeated experience of feeling rejected—even when their partners are not meaning to reject them—leads them to respond by being critical of their partners.

To help clarify how mentalizing can be affected by attachment-related anxiety, consider the way Sydney—a woman with a strong pre-occupied style—reacts after a blind date ignores her obvious willingness to meet again. Understandably, she is unhappy about this. However, because of her weak ability to mentalize, she equates the feeling of rejection with her being flawed and unworthy of love. She feels despair and isolates herself. However, if her attachment-related anxiety were less intense, her ability to understand the situation with more perspective might not be so impaired. She could feel hurt while recognizing that not everyone clicks—and that being rejected does not make her a reject. She might even remember that there are men she's liked or respected in the past who did not interest her romantically.

While strengthening her ability to mentalize can help Sydney to open up positive ways of thinking about herself and her relationships, it unfortunately does not automatically relieve distress. All too often people think that they should no longer be upset once they understand their circumstance. In my clinical practice, it is not unusual for patients to say something like, "I know I'm always afraid of being judged because my father was cruel when I was a child. But that was a long time ago and he's dead now. So why can't I just get over it already?" The answer is that some things in life are painful, and no amount of understanding will change that. But learning to respond with self-compassion can soothe that hurt and help you move forward in life.

Mentalizing can sound complicated; and in some ways it is. But you already practice it in your life when considering your emotions as you think about why you do what you do, or why others do what they do. In the next chapter I will offer exercises to specifically develop your mentalizing ability.

Self-Compassion

Self-awareness—which includes awareness of emotions, awareness of thoughts, and mentalizing—is a powerful tool, but it can't help you by itself. So let's take a look at the other half of the formula for making effective, lasting change—self-compassion.

People don't just *understand* themselves or *have* emotions or *think* thoughts; they *relate to* these experiences. When people accept themselves and befriend their emotions, it is natural for them to treat themselves with kindness and relate to themselves with *self-compassion*. Although people don't talk much about *self*-compassion, they often do talk about compassion, which is something you feel for someone else who is in pain. It involves putting yourself in someone else's shoes, or having empathy, and wanting to alleviate their suffering. Self-compassion is simply taking that same stance with yourself.

Researcher Kristin Neff (2008) is at the forefront of exploring self-compassion and its implications. She defines it as having three main parts: *self-kindness*, *common humanity*, and *mindfulness*.

Self-Kindness

This is just what it sounds like—being kind to yourself. People who embrace this quality are gentle with themselves when they experience pain, failure, or inadequacy. Rather than becoming angry with or critical of themselves in these circumstances, they respond with understanding and gentleness. They have a desire to treat themselves well, not just to fulfill immediate gratification, but to be healthy, happy people for the long term. So, while they are kind and accepting of themselves in the moment, they are also motivated to change for the better.

These last points are extremely important. Many people fear that self-kindness might lead to being lazy or complacent, or letting themselves off the hook too easily. But true self-compassion—like compassion in general—is not merely a pursuit of immediate gratification. Consider some well-known compassionate people whom you probably think of with respect: Buddha, Gandhi, Jesus, Martin Luther King Jr.,

Mother Teresa, Nelson Mandela. Their great compassion inspired them to work persistently in helping others experience a greater sense of well-being—and achieving ambitious goals can be part of that. In the same way, *self*-compassion will naturally inspire you to pursue inner growth.

It's also important to understand that being self-kind does not mean being selfish. When you are self-kind, you care very much about other people as well as about your own needs. However, this sometimes means focusing on your own pain first. Christopher Germer (2009, 89) expresses this well in his book *The Mindful Path to Self-Compassion*: "In a room full of people, it makes sense to help the person who's suffering the most, the one we know best, the one we're most capable of helping. Sometimes that person is you..."

Common Humanity

This is the recognition that all people share common experiences, such as pain and suffering, weaknesses and imperfections. By feeling connected to others in this way, people feel less isolated and less lonely. They realize that their problems are just part of being human, and that these difficulties do not mean that there is something essentially wrong with them. So rather than being mired in self-pity, those with a strong sense of common humanity tend to feel more okay (though not necessarily happy) about their struggles.

Mindfulness

This is a nonjudgmental awareness of thoughts and feelings without attachment to them. Unlike the discussion of awareness of thoughts and feelings in the "Self-Awareness" section above, mindfulness focuses more on the process of awareness—how you approach and treat your experiences—than on exploring and differentiating the experiences themselves. When you are mindful, you are truly in the moment. You accept experiences without the need to deny, suppress, or exaggerate them. You also have perspective on your experiences, more self-compassion, and a greater sense of well-being during stressful times.

The benefits of mindfulness become especially apparent when you consider what happens when people are *not* mindful. For instance, people who are easily triggered to feel overwhelmed with a sense of rejection often lose perspective and overly identify with their thoughts and feelings. They react by being clingy or lashing out in anger. In both cases, they push their partners further away—the opposite of the closeness that they really crave. And if they try to suppress their negative feelings, those feelings often come back with even greater intensity. By contrast, if these people learned to be more mindful, they would feel less overwhelmed, even amid distressing feelings, and could understand themselves and their reactions better. As a result, they could respond in healthier, more constructive ways—such as by talking with their partners about their struggles and directly asking for reassurance (Wallin, 2007).

As Neff (2008) emphasizes, self-compassion cannot occur without self-kindness, common humanity, *and* mindfulness. People must experience self-kindness; they must be motivated to act on their own behalf toward a sense of well-being. They must understand and feel that they are part of a common humanity in which every person struggles just as they do. And, finally, they must be mindful so that they can be aware of their experiences without being overwhelmed by them. Together, these three elements can help you to nurture a positive sense of yourself, a greater sense of security with your partner, and a more effective way to address issues in your relationship.

Exercise: What's Your Level of Self-Compassion?

Given the importance of self-compassion in alleviating attachment-related anxiety, you may find it helpful to assess yourself in each of the elements that make it up: self-kindness, common humanity, and mindfulness. On a scale of 1-5, rate how well you identify with the statements in an area. Then divide this by the number of statements in each area to get your final rating for the area.

1	2	3	4	5
Not at all				Completely

Self-Kindness

_____ You are accepting and gentle with yourself in response to your imperfections or inadequacies.

_____ You are accepting and gentle with yourself when you make mistakes.

_____ You are caring and nurture yourself when you are hurting or emotionally upset.

_____ You want to treat yourself well so you can be happy in the long term.

Total: _____ ÷ 4 = _____

Common Humanity

_____ You believe others have weaknesses, imperfections, or inadequacies just like you do.

_____ You can see your struggles as part of being human; you realize that you are not alone in them.

_____ When upset, you can remember that other people sometimes have similar struggles and feelings.

_____ Remembering that other people sometimes have similar struggles and feelings helps you to feel less alone.

Total: _____ ÷ 4 = _____

Mindfulness

_____ You can accept your thoughts and feelings without judging them—even when upset.

_____ You can accept your thoughts and feelings without denying, suppressing, or exaggerating them.

_____ You can experience your emotions without becoming overly identified with them and losing perspective.

_____ When upset or during challenging times, you try to maintain a healthy perspective.

Total: _____ ÷ 4 = _____

The higher your score for an area (the highest score being a 5), the stronger you are in it. Keep these scores in mind when you consider the exercises in chapter 7: Creating Self-Compassion. For any areas of weakness, you might choose to focus more on the exercises that target strengthening them.

♡

Benefits of Self-Compassion

To better understand the benefits of self-compassion, consider this example: Dan is at a party with his date Jill and her friends. He doesn't know much about art, which is what most of their careers or interests seem to revolve around. Rather than risk losing Jill's respect by saying the wrong thing, he totally shuts down and doesn't say a word. *He relates to his experience of confusion with fear of being seen as incompetent.* By contrast, Lucas—who is with his girlfriend Sophie at the opening of an art show, though he knows little about art—isn't worried about being viewed as incompetent. He accepts that all people have strengths and weaknesses. *He relates to his confusion about how to proceed by acknowledging his limitations.* So he asks thoughtful questions, appreciates the insights offered, and feels good about the knowledge he gains. Not surprisingly, Dan wins no allies among Jill's friends, who view him as distant; while Lucas enjoys a pleasant evening with Sophie and her friends, who enjoy sharing their expertise with a willing and eager audience.

Lucas, who is securely attached, enjoyed a childhood of feeling accepted and comforted by his parents. He took in all of these positive interactions and developed a mental representation of his parents (his attachment figures). This mental representation naturally "steps in" when, as an adult, he feels uncomfortable or threatened in any way, reassuring him that he is a worthy person.

By contrast, Dan was raised by loving parents, but they were not able to consistently comfort his anxieties as a child. Still, he generally felt happy in relationships until his last year of college, when he developed his first serious relationship with Susan. She was highly critical and eventually cheated on him with his friend; and then she dumped him. Since that time—especially with women—he has tended to be self-critical, to feel extremely anxious with women, and to feel particularly fearful of, and vulnerable to, rejection. His way of coping with this was to keep quiet so that he didn't reveal his inadequacies and could hopefully avoid rejection. This often backfired because women felt they couldn't connect with him.

If—like Dan—you tend to doubt your worth and be judgmental of yourself, research in self-compassion offers you some good news. There's strong evidence that self-compassion is related to the ability to see reality more objectively, have insight, and be motivated to achieve personal growth—all of which can help you overcome your tendency to self-verify your attachment-related anxiety. In support of this, there's also evidence that self-compassion can help you to feel more socially connected, more satisfied with life, and to have a greater sense of well-being (Baera, Lykins, and Peters, 2012; Barnard and Curry, 2011).

Importantly, with self-compassion, you feel worthy of happiness, love, and affection even after failure, or when facing your limitations or weaknesses. So, in a sense, you can't lose. You can put yourself out there, risk failure, wrestle with personal demons, and continue to view yourself positively as someone who is learning and growing. The result is a happier you with greater chances for a happier relationship. (I say greater *chances* for a happier relationship because, no matter what you do, you still need your partner to work with you to nurture a successful relationship.)

The Healing Power of Compassionate Self-Awareness

If you find it hard to be compassionate toward your own struggles, then you need to develop compassionate self-awareness. Each part of compassionate self-awareness provides an essential element to getting unstuck. To review, the main elements are self-awareness and self-compassion.

Self-Awareness

Awareness of emotions

- Identification of your emotions

- Conscious experience of your emotions

Awareness of thoughts

- Objective awareness of thoughts

- Allowing yourself to see how you perpetuate your attachment-related anxiety

Mentalizing

- Maintaining intellectual perspective about yourself while remaining emotionally connected to your experiences

- A reflective stance that allows you to consider possible reasons for your emotions, thoughts, and behaviors, as well as those of your partner

- Understanding how your way of perceiving yourself and your partner might be biased

Self-Compassion

- Acceptance of yourself

- Compassionate response to your distress

People high in self-compassion go through times of pain and difficulty just like everyone else. They need help from others; they need connection, support, and advice. However, they have several distinct advantages. They are more accepting of themselves; they are better at nurturing healthy relationships; they can make better use of appropriate advice or feedback when they make mistakes or are struggling with particular problems; and they are more resilient.

If you do not have much self-compassion, you—unfortunately—cannot just will it to exist. However, through compassionate self-awareness, you can develop it and nurture a greater happiness within yourself and within your relationship. If you are not in a relationship, it can still help you to feel positively about yourself, as well as to approach finding a partner in a more effective way.

To clarify how this works, consider Peter. He is a forty-five-year-old bachelor who would like to marry. When he meets Amanda, he is enamored of her and decides to totally devote himself to this new relationship. He pours himself out to her, hopeful that she will accept and love him. He is able to be so open, in part, because he overrides and tries to ignore his fears that she might reject him. With time, however, he is aware that he's beginning to feel distant from her (awareness of emotions). He's conscious of being critical of her. He thinks things like, "She can be really annoying," or "It's not much fun spending time with her" (awareness of thoughts). At first he thinks that maybe there's just not enough chemistry. But when she cannot get together with him one night, he misses her desperately, fears she'll leave, and is anxious to win her love again (awareness of emotions and thoughts). At that point he realizes (with the help of mentalizing) that the problem is not a lack of chemistry between them. He can see that he has instinctively protected himself from getting hurt by being critical of her. With this insight, he can view his feelings and actions as understandable and human (self-compassion). So rather than ending the relationship as he had been considering, he has a new option—to face his fear of rejection. After much support and encouragement from friends, he talks to her about this fear, allowing himself to be truly vulnerable. This leads to them working together on building emotional intimacy—a connection beyond just sharing the details of their lives.

Without awareness of thoughts and feelings, mentalizing, and self-compassion, Peter's story might not have ended so well. He might have concluded that there was simply no chemistry and broken up with Amanda. Or even if they had married, he would most likely have vacillated between being critical and distant, on one hand, and passionately engaged in trying to win her over or reassure himself of her love, on the other. Alternatively, *she* might have felt a lack of connection with him and eventually broken off the relationship. If he were still unaware of his struggle when she did this, he would have been left confused, unable to understand what went wrong. And if this was a long-standing pattern for him, he might then have questioned what was wrong with him that was constantly causing him to be rejected.

Compassionate self-awareness is effective because it provides a way for people to work *with* their inner conflicts, as Peter did. If you are extremely upset about some issues in your relationship, you or your partner demanding that you "stop worrying" won't fix anything. It might even intensify your feelings—turning them into a tsunami that will overwhelm any positive effort to address the problems at hand. At times like this, compassionate self-awareness can help you to understand your struggles and approach them in a caring, gentle manner—ultimately allowing you to nurture the relationship you want.

I can think of no more succinct or more eloquent way to describe compassionate self-awareness than this statement (widely attributed to playwright August Wilson): "Confront the dark parts of yourself, and work to banish them with illumination and forgiveness. Your willingness to wrestle with your demons will cause your angels to sing. Use the pain as fuel, as a reminder of your strength."

In the next two chapters, I will help you with just that. Chapter 6 provides guidance for how to illuminate your inner experiences—the dark and not so dark ones. Chapter 7 offers suggestions for learning to approach yourself with forgiveness and compassion.

Chapter 6

Developing Self-Awareness

As I've explained, you have good reasons for maintaining your attachment-related anxiety—it can feel like a matter of survival. If you try to reduce this anxiety, your resistance will naturally run deep. This is true even if you consciously want to change and would be healthier for it. So if you are intent on improving your relationship, or searching for one, approach it diplomatically. Expect inner resistance and plan to persist. Instead of trying to overpower (or bully) yourself with demands to be different, try to "make friends" with your experiences. As with any new friends, you will earnestly try to get to know and understand them. Also, remember that those aspects of you that are holding on to attachment-related anxiety are trying to protect you—so engage with them sensitively.

Begin by opening yourself up to the idea of changing. Then you can move on to becoming more aware and accepting of your emotions, gaining awareness and perspective regarding your thoughts, and increasing your ability to mentalize. The sections below offer ways to develop in each of these areas. Try the exercises that seem to touch on where you need to—and are ready to—grow. Do them in whatever order seems to be most helpful, and repeat exercises as you see fit. Be alert to a strong desire *not* to do an exercise or to an aversion to thinking about some particular section. That could be a misguided effort by your unconscious to protect you, and might reveal an important area that you need to work on. So give serious consideration to what that section is addressing and to trying the exercise in it.

Resist the temptation to "push through the book" without really absorbing what the exercises have to offer. Feel free to work on any particular exercise for a while, or even to return to that exercise later after reading on.

Facing Your Ambivalence

To develop a secure romantic relationship, it helps to be aware of your ambivalence toward opening yourself up to the vulnerability that this goal invariably brings. It's this awareness that can help you to see when and how your attachment-related anxiety prevents you from improving your relationship.

For instance, Andy knew that communication is important in relationships, so he forced himself to talk with his wife about her recently being distant. However, because he failed to acknowledge just how threatened he felt, he unconsciously protected himself by delivering the message in a hostile and accusatory manner ("We might as well not even be married. Honestly, you're of no use to me!"). This only served to create more distance. Had he been more aware of wanting to talk but also wanting to avoid getting hurt, he would have had the opportunity to talk about his fear, which would have been more likely to elicit a caring response from his wife.

By facing your ambivalence, you are also facing your fears that you are unworthy of love (or that your partner might see you this way), and that you might lose the relationship you want so much. This is no small task. But by doing it, you will notice when you delay or self-sabotage attempts to improve your love life.

As you gain this awareness, approach your fears and anxieties gently. Take small steps. Prepare yourself for change by consciously working with your ambivalence. Do this in whatever way works for you, such as giving yourself time to think about your struggles, journaling, talking with a supportive friend, or expressing your struggles creatively, perhaps by painting or writing poetry.

It's very important to understand that greater self-awareness does not mean you have to act any differently. So remove this pressure from yourself. For instance, acknowledging that you feel disrespected by your partner does not mean you *must* leave her. However, when you are caught in a bad pattern, greater awareness will help you to see how your patterns of behavior are painful. This increases the chances that you will *want* to do something differently. To this end, it might help to talk with someone you trust about your problems, or to read a good self-help book. In some cases, you might even find inspiration in a novel or movie. For instance, watching the movie *Silver Linings Playbook* (2012) might help you to feel that you can find love and happiness even with your emotional struggles.

Facing ambivalence is something you'll need to do repeatedly as you challenge yourself to become more secure and to respond differently along the way in relationships. But at each of these times, when you are ready to take the next step, whatever it is, just do it. Be careful not to fall into the trap of thinking...and rethinking...*and rethinking* about your situation. Remember the adage, "Strike while the iron is hot"? Now's the time to apply it.

Nurturing Awareness of Emotions

People have difficulty identifying their emotions for many reasons. If you have trouble with this, it may be because you are out of touch with them. Or perhaps you don't know the words to best describe them. Or you might be focusing more on your thinking. Or glossing over your emotions with general descriptions, such as "upset" or "bothered."

If you have attachment-related anxiety, you are likely to find that your emotions frequently build in intensity and seem to meld together, leaving you feeling overwhelmed by one large, unidentifiable mass of emotion. Simply acknowledging and labeling emotions can deactivate and calm the amygdala, the part of your brain that triggers your intense distress.

By completing the next exercise, "Identifying Your Emotions," you can learn to identify and differentiate your emotions. In doing so, you'll also lessen their intensity and your distress—which will, in turn, enable you to learn to tolerate them better. Then you'll be in a better position to nurture a closer relationship by communicating them to your partner in a productive way.

In going through this process, it is important that you develop the ability to both open up to your emotions *and* close yourself off to them. For instance, you can help yourself really feel your fear of rejection, which will feel "right" in that it is your genuine experience. But then, after some time of connecting with that experience, you might find that you are just digging yourself deeper into a depressive hole, or creating a greater sense of emotional chaos. I have found in my clinical experience that people usually have a sense of when they are productively connecting with their emotions versus just making themselves more upset. The idea is that, just as with any new skill, you want to stay in the gray zone—a little beyond what is comfortable, but not so far out that you are overreaching. When experiencing your emotions becomes counterproductive, it's time to let go of this process and engage in something comforting—maybe lunch with a friend, watching a movie, or enjoying a walk in the park.

Exercise: Identifying Your Emotions

You can find clues to your emotions in the current situation, your bodily sensations, and your behaviors. So monitor these on a daily basis. If you tend to do well with structured help, make a chart with a column for each of these areas, as described below. Or, if you prefer, simply think about the areas—it can help to do this at prescribed times, such as in the morning or at meals. You might also talk about them with a trusted friend or your partner.

Although I discussed the difference between thoughts and feelings in the last chapter, the separation between these two things is not absolute. People's thoughts or perceptions of a situation often affect their emotions. For instance, you may feel deeply sad when you reflect on your perception of yourself as having no value to others. In this case, it is more accurate to say that you feel "worthless" or "pathetic" than to label your emotion as "sad." Even though these words reflect thoughts or judgments, they also express an emotional experience. Similarly, after finding out that your spouse has had an affair, your hurt and anger would mix with your thoughts to leave you feeling betrayed. So as you consider your emotions, you might find that they are influenced or somehow intermingled with your thoughts.

Consider the chart below. Use it, and the explanation of it that follows, to guide your thinking or as an example for setting up your own chart.

CHART 1
(EXERCISE: IDENTIFYING YOUR EMOTIONS)

Date	3/5
Situation	John called and said he won't be home for dinner—third time this week
Sensations	Tightness in my chest, headache soon after we talked
Behaviors	Hung up quickly; cried
Thoughts	It's not okay for him to keep doing this. What am I doing wrong to make him not want to come home? Is he having an affair?
Emotions	Frustrated, angry, anxious, afraid he'll leave me, hurt, betrayed

Date: By recording the date, you can help keep track of patterns in your emotions, especially if you return to this exercise at different times.

Situation: Make note of the situation when you feel distressed. For instance, you might notice that your husband is not home for dinner for the third time this week, and that he only let you know he'd be late as an afterthought when you phoned him.

Sensations: Pay attention to how you feel in your body. For instance, when you learned that your husband was going to be home late, you felt tight in your chest and even developed a headache soon afterward. In other situations, you might feel hot, dizzy, or shaky, or you might have "butterflies" in your stomach.

Behaviors: Note what you did in response to the situation. In our example, you might write down that you got off the phone quickly and then cried—or threw something.

Thoughts: Note your thoughts about the situation, yourself, and your partner. So, in this column you might write, "It's not okay for him to keep doing this. I wonder what I'm doing wrong that's pushing him away. I think he might be having an affair."

Emotions: As you attend to your sensations, behaviors, and thoughts, do particular emotions arise? Rather than trying to force a label of what you think you "should" be feeling, try letting the names of the emotions bubble up. For instance, you might write, "Frustration, anger, anxiety, fear of rejection, hurt, betrayal."

If this proves too difficult, consult the list of emotions in the chart that follows. To be clear, this list includes labels for basic emotions (such as joyful, angry, and afraid); combinations of emotions (surprised + sad = disappointed); and combinations of emotions and thoughts (joyful + perceived success = proud). I provide all of these combinations to help you recognize the many nuances of the emotions that you might feel. So see which ones you connect with. You might even want to copy this chart and keep it handy throughout your day. Remember that you might be experiencing a number of emotions—even some that conflict with each other.

By identifying your emotions, you are acknowledging your experience. This is fundamental in understanding yourself, managing your feelings effectively, and communicating with your partner in a way that enables him to understand you—and hopefully to connect with you, too. So, especially if you struggle with identifying your emotions, this exercise is well worth practicing.

List of Emotions

HAPPY

At ease	Calm	Optimistic
Ecstatic	Energetic	Satisfied
Hopeful	Inspired	Wonderful
Pleased	Relaxed	Content
Thankful	Cheerful	Glad
Blissful	Excited	Peaceful
Elated	Lighthearted	Serene
Humorous	Relieved	Delighted
Proud	Comfortable	Grateful
Tranquil	Exhilarated	Playful

Spirited

COMPETENT

	Privileged	Invincible
Adept	Strong	Secure
Capable	Arrogant	Together
Independent	Confident	Cocky
Powerful	Inspired	Important
Self-reliant	Savvy	Invulnerable
Adequate	Thoughtful	Self-assured
Composed	Brave	Worthy
Indestructible	Courageous	

VALUED

Accepted	Cherished	Favored
Belonging	Loved	Understood
Included	Revered	Desirable
Respected	Wanted	Desired
Worshipped	Adored	Idolized
Admired	Appreciated	Validated

LOVING

Affectionate	Adoring	Enchanted
Attracted	Desirous	Infatuated
Fond	Horny	Passionate
Longing	Lustful	
Yearning	Aroused	

CARING

Compassionate	Tender	Liking
Connected	Concerned	Warm
Forgiving	Empathic	

INTERESTED

Absorbed	Eager	Resolute
Challenged	Fervent	Ardent
Determined	Motivated	Dedicated
Fascinated	Anticipating	Enthusiastic
Intrigued	Curious	Intent
Addicted	Engrossed	
Committed	Focused	

VINDICATED

Absolved	Forgiven	Redeemed
Appeased		

UNHAPPY

Agonized	Disillusioned	Melancholy
Discontented	Jealous	Sad
Hurt	Pessimistic	Despondent
Negative	Suspicious	Grief-stricken
Stressed	Crushed	Miserable
Alone	Dissatisfied	Shameful
Discouraged	Lonely	Detached
Inadequate	Regretful	Guilty
Pained	Tortured	Moody
Stubborn	Dark	Somber
Anguished	Envious	Disappointed
Disheartened	Low	Heartbroken
Inferior	Remorseful	Needy
Pathetic	Withdrawn	Startled
Sullen	Depressed	
Blue	Gloomy	

INSECURE

Awkward	Lost	Unsure
Confused	Torn	Common
Indecisive	Unfocused	Foolish
Surprised	Bewildered	Silly
Uncomfortable	Embarrassed	Uneasy
Baffled	Puzzled	Worthless
Disoriented	Uncertain	

OVERWHELMED

Burdened	Worn down	Obliterated
Despairing	Worn out	Useless
Hopeless	Confused	Defeated
Pressured	Disorganized	Helpless
Thwarted	Obligated	Powerless
Compelled	Trapped	Weak
Devastated	Consumed	
Impotent	Exhausted	

UNLOVED

Abandoned	Deserted	Judged
Criticized	Ignored	Rejected
Hated	Oppressed	Victimized
Lonely	Unsupported	Betrayed
Singled out	Alone	Disparaged
Aching	Discarded	Labeled
Cut off	Insignificant	Repulsive
Humiliated	Overlooked	Chastised
Misunderstood	Used	Excluded
Unlovable	Belittled	Left out
Alienated	Disgraced	Shamed

FEARFUL

Afraid	Anxious	Cautious
Cowardly	Distrustful	Dreading
Frightened	Horrified	Nervous
Paranoid	Scared	Suspicious
Terrified	Vulnerable	Concerned
Alarmed	Apprehensive	Exposed
Defenseless	Doubtful	Panicked
Hesitant	Hysterical	Tense
Petrified	Shaky	
Timid	Worried	

ANGRY

Aggressive	Outraged	Livid
Defiant	Appalled	Resentful
Fuming	Disgusted	Contemptuous
Infuriated	Hostile	Frustrated
Offended	Irritated	Indignant
Annoyed	Repulsed	Mad
Disdainful	Bitter	Scornful
Furious	Enraged	
Irate	Incensed	

INDIFFERENT

Ambivalent	Apathetic	Bored
Complacent	Flat	Lackadaisical
Lazy	Lethargic	Numb
Passive	Unmotivated	

SURPRISED

Amazed	Astonished	Shocked

♡

Tolerating Your Emotions

As you open up to self-awareness, it is essential that you be able to tolerate your emotions. You must be able to endure emotional distress while resisting the urge to try to make it immediately disappear, which would prevent you from fully connecting with, understanding, and coming to terms with the experience. Neural plasticity—the ability of the brain to change—is what enables this working-through process to help you eventually relate differently to your emotions.

You can increase tolerance of your emotions by exposing yourself to them, but carefully, and not so much that you feel overwhelmed. You can do this through mindfulness and meditation, which I will discuss in depth in chapter 8. You can also do it by approaching your emotions with curiosity.

Because being curious about your experiences means wanting to know more about them, such curiosity will naturally help you to stay open to your emotions, despite some anxiety. This, in turn, will enable you to explore them more thoroughly, and to find and integrate meaning from your newly recognized feelings. This positive focus can help you to develop a greater tolerance for distressing emotions. One way to develop curiosity is by simply completing the previous exercise, "Identifying Your Emotions"—but with a decision to approach it with an open and curious mind.

Exercise: Befriending Your Emotions

As you develop an ability to tolerate your emotions, you can work on being more open to them—and even befriending them. To befriend your emotions is to invite them into your life because you see value in them. No, you wouldn't actively want to feel upset; but you could be grateful for the benefits that a particular situation and its related emotions bring to your life. For instance, you might appreciate your loneliness because it motivates you to get moving on trying to meet new people or a new special someone.

You can begin the process by thinking about specific emotional situations and considering the following:

- Do your emotions help you understand the situation or your interaction better?

- Are your emotions a warning that there is a problem you need to attend to?

- Are your emotions an expression of empathy, helping you connect with your partner or others?

Through these questions you can approach your emotions as you would a friend—with an open heart. It helps to remember that emotions are part of being human, even when they are painful. It also helps to be patient with yourself; learning to befriend your emotions can be a long-term project and a skill that you will have to practice for the rest of your life.

♡

Transforming Your Thoughts with Greater Awareness

As explained in the last chapter, your thoughts influence you on many levels. If you pay attention to, and increase your awareness of, your attachment-related anxious thoughts and their effects, you might begin to question them. Sometimes you can simply substitute new, healthier thinking for the old, self-destructive thoughts.

For instance, you might choose to focus on your tendency to repeat, "I haven't had a girlfriend in so long; I'm such a loser." You can start by being aware of every time you say this to yourself, and then replace that thought with a more positive message: "I've had a dry spell for a while, but I've been in relationships before and I can find someone special again." If you believe this new message at all, you might help yourself to think it more automatically by consciously practicing it.

Don't be hard on yourself if this doesn't work. The approach has its limits. If the new statement is in direct conflict with your self-perceptions, repeating it will never be wholly convincing, just as you will never convince yourself that night is day, no matter how many times you label the moon as the sun.

What's most important now is that you become more aware of your thoughts and how they affect you. By doing this you are establishing a solid foundation for understanding your feelings and beliefs about yourself and your relationships, and for relating differently to those feelings and beliefs. For instance, again consider awareness of having the frequent thought, "I haven't had a girlfriend in so long; I'm such a loser." You might also come to realize that every time you have that thought, it's as if you are giving yourself an injection of despair and hopelessness. Once you realize this, you have a better understanding of how your emotions work. Making this connection is an important step in relating more positively to yourself.

Exercise: Changing Your "Thought Bubble"

Your negative thoughts—either in the form of self-criticisms or in the form of perceptions that your partner does not sufficiently value you—perpetuate your attachment-related anxiety. To directly change these thoughts, or at least lessen their effect on you, complete the chart on the following page.

As with so much else I've addressed, it's very important to be patient with yourself. You are working to change a way of being that has probably been with you since childhood, so it will take time to establish a new way of thinking and feeling. Spend some time reviewing the chart. Journal about it. Talk with a supportive friend. Think about it until you understand the ways that your thinking has *previously* caused problems in yourself and your relationships—and until you are conscious of when and how your thinking is *currently* creating problems for you.

To begin, make a chart that you can fill in each day. Label five columns: Date, Situation, Attachment-Related Anxious Thoughts (related to your partner and you), Effects of Thoughts on Feelings and Behaviors, and Disconfirming Evidence.

CHART 2 EXERCISE:
CHANGING YOUR "THOUGHT BUBBLE"

Date	2/19
Situation	Patrick met his friends out at a bar
Attachment-Related Anxious Thoughts (related to you, and to your partner)	Him: He wants to go out with his friends so he can look for someone he likes better than me; I can't trust him; he just wants to be with his friends and doesn't care about me Me: I'm not interesting enough; I'm not pretty enough
Effects of Thoughts on Feelings and Behaviors	Feelings: Anxious, jealous, afraid of him leaving me, angry with him, inadequate Behaviors: Check his cell phone when he's home and not looking; call him a lot when he's out
Disconfirming Evidence	He's always making plans for us to go out; he is thoughtful and tells me he cares (my logic is flawed); Lori's boyfriend goes out with his friends and I don't think he's getting ready to leave her; I have friends who like talking with me and find me interesting and fun to be with

Date: Noting the date will help you keep track of patterns, especially if you complete this during different periods of time.

Situation: Write down details about the situation related to your current, past, or potential partner that triggered you to become upset. For instance, you might be upset when your boyfriend goes out with the guys.

Attachment-Related Anxious Thoughts: Ask yourself, "What thoughts reinforce my attachment-related anxiety?" It can be helpful to note thoughts related both to yourself and to your partner. Some examples are:

- If only I were more interesting, he'd feel stronger about our relationship and spend time with me instead of the guys.

- If only I were prettier, he might want to stay with me.

- He'll leave once he really gets to know me, or once he finds someone better.

- He doesn't want to hang out with me, so there must be something wrong with me.

- He doesn't care how I feel.

Effects of Thoughts on Feelings and Behaviors: Once you are clear about what you say to yourself, think about how this makes you feel, and how it influences your behaviors. For instance, if you are always thinking about how your boyfriend is going to leave you, you will probably feel frequent anxiety and easily triggered jealousy, and may act possessively. This is a no-win situation. If he really is committed to the relationship, you won't see this and will be unhappy. If he isn't committed, you might still cling to the relationship, remaining immersed in a desperate need to prove your value to him.

Disconfirming Evidence: Pay attention to how your reactions unfold in daily life and how they are a consequence of your flawed thinking rather than the likely reality of your situation. Your tendency to self-verify attachment-related anxiety can make this a tricky assessment. But try playing devil's advocate with yourself. For instance, if you worry that your boyfriend's going out with the guys means he's not very interested you, you might consider these questions:

- What evidence is there for the idea that he might be happy with me? (For instance, he tells me he loves me; he texts or calls me every day; he took care of me when I was sick.)

- In what ways am I critical of myself? (For instance, I view myself as boring or stupid for thinking he'd want a future with me.)

- If my best friend were in the same situation, would I think the same thing about her and her situation? If not, what *would* I think? (For instance, I'd think his wanting to go out with the guys has nothing to do with how interesting she is. He shows her that he cares, so it's clear that he wants to be with her.)

What you are looking for is, as they say in court, "a shadow of a doubt" for you to use as a reason for considering other ways of thinking about yourself and your partner. If there is no realistic shadow of a doubt about your negative perceptions of your partner, it may be time to address them with him—or to move on. If you are unable to take action in either of these ways, or if you have no realistic doubt about your negative self-perceptions, you will benefit from adding self-compassion to your developing self-awareness. If that is the case, you may simply move on to the next section.

If the disconfirming evidence does instill some real doubt and the realization of the negative effects of your thinking, you might naturally develop a more positive perspective as you continue to fill out the chart. You can help this process along by actively reminding yourself of the disconfirming evidence when you are aware of mounting attachment-related anxiety. Choose to focus on the more positive and realistic ways of seeing your situation. For instance, when you feel anxious about your boyfriend leaving, you might note that he texts you daily and seems happy to see you when you go out together.

If your attachment-related anxious thoughts remain entrenched, or change seems to be coming too slowly, you might need a little more help. You can find this help by actively developing your capacity for self-compassion, which I will discuss in the next chapter.

♡

Mentalizing

Mentalizing involves a clarity of heart and mind. It's an emotionally connected, intellectual understanding of why you and your partner feel and act as you do. With it, you can reverse your usual self-centered perceptions by seeing yourself from the outside and understanding your partner from the inside. More specifically, it provides you with insight that helps you to understand:

- The causes of distress

- The impact of growing up in your "family of origin" (your mother, father, siblings) on your relationship

- The impact of other experiences on your relationship

- The obstacles to a healthier, more intimate relationship

- The reasons you become unreasonably upset at times

Remember that your attachment-related anxiety is associated with your instinct to survive. So, given its importance, it can sometimes overwhelm you and make mentalizing particularly difficult. However, you can gain access to insights about your mental states, or those of your partner, by considering thoughts, feelings, and behaviors. For instance, you might be tipped off to your level of anger with your partner by your spontaneous outburst or your fantasy of hitting her. You can also improve your mentalizing by consciously "playing" with different ideas, developing stories about why you are feeling and acting some particular way, or why your partner is. Feedback from your partner or trusted others can help in this process. But gaining this kind of perspective is not easy, so, again, be patient. Expect it to take time and effort. If it's just too hard, consider seeing a therapist who can help you.

Exercise: Choose to Be Curious

One of the best ways to strengthen your ability to mentalize is to consciously become more curious about yourself or your partner. In this exercise, you will focus on developing different ways of viewing your partner. Importantly, the goal is to consider multiple views, not just to find the "right" one. This will help you to develop a style of remaining open to possibilities rather than instantly clamping down on them with one judgment, like a steel trap. Do this in four steps:

1. *Choose a situation.* Pick some behavior or interaction—positive or negative—to focus on that you have questions about, or that you *could* be wrong about.

   Example: Sybil's neighbor Russ invited her out on a date. Because she struggles with low self-esteem and because he knew she hadn't gone out with anyone in some time, she figured that it was a "pity date."

2. *Check in with what you are feeling and thinking.* Do a thorough job of this—you might even want to consult the "Identifying Your Emotions" exercise earlier in this chapter.

   Example: Sybil might first be aware of feeling insecure, confused, afraid, and anxious. Then she might realize that, in spite of herself, she was excited, felt wanted, was attracted to Russ, and was intrigued by the possibility of a relationship. She might also realize that she was critical of herself—thinking she was a fool and feeling angry that she had gotten her hopes up.

3. *Consider possible explanations.* Once you can connect with and identify your emotions and thoughts, consider the possible reasons why the incident happened, using what you know about yourself and your partner.

   Example: Sybil might think that Russ possibly asked her out because he was bored, because he pitied her, because he wanted to just be going out as friends, or—maybe—because he liked her.

4. *Find out the truth.* For the purposes of this exercise, this last step is not necessarily very important—that is, what's essential here is not that you guess correctly about the motivations of your partner. Instead, the purpose of this exercise is to open yourself up to considering possibilities as you remain connected with how you feel. That said, once you are more open, you might find an answer that

is supported by the evidence around you and that resonates inside you as accurate, even if it is not comfortable.

Example: While Sybil might choose not to ask Russ outright why he asked her out—despite really wanting to—she could look for signs of his intentions. For instance, it would mean one thing if he mentioned that his other friends were all out of town this weekend, but quite another if he confessed that he found her attractive and had wanted to ask her out for a long time.

Note: The examples in this exercise focused on trying to understand someone else. But you can also complete this exercise by focusing on yourself. As I've noted, we can be blind to our own intentions and struggles.

♡

Exercise: Getting to Know Your Partner from the Inside Out

Mentalizing can help you to become emotionally closer to your partner because it can give you a window into her world. It does this by providing you with a more detailed understanding of her experience.

Your goal is to really see the world through your partner's eyes, including what she observed, felt, and thought. Keep in mind that you don't have to agree. Also, you don't want a grainy home-movie view, but rather more of a highdefinition, being-in-her-shoes experience.

Keep the following in mind when your partner is talking with you about an experience (it could be anything from going fishing to mourning the death of a parent).

DO:

• Give her all of your attention—no multitasking.

• Tell your partner you're interested in hearing about the topic.

- At appropriate times, ask for more detail or explanation so you can really "get it"—the facts *and* her thoughts *and* her feelings.

- Note nonverbal cues for a better sense of the intensity and quality of her experience.

- Be open to her perspective, particularly when it doesn't match yours.

DON'T:

- Multitask—not even to just look at that incoming text.

- Interrupt, unless you are confused and need clarification.

- Assume you know what she is thinking or feeling.

- Try to solve a problem (unless you are asked to).

- Tell her she's wrong about the facts or her experience.

With time, your efforts will pay off. You will feel closer to your partner and she will feel closer to you. This will also go a long way toward alleviating any unnecessary fears of rejection.

♡

Final Thoughts on Self-Awareness

Self-awareness requires patience. It must occur at an optimal level of tension between newly developing awareness and old perceptions of yourself and your partner. Otherwise, self-verification will override your new awareness, whether it be thoughts, feelings, or mentalizing.

So, remind yourself of this. Think, journal, complete the exercises in this book, talk with your partner, and share with other trusted family and friends. Above all, persist in your exploration of new ways of connecting with your own experience and with your partner.

Chapter 7

Creating Self-Compassion

Becoming consciously aware of your biases about yourself and your partner is not an easy process. The discomfort it causes can trigger you to automatically seek reassurance by turning from your growing awareness back to your old biases—those insecure patterns of attachment. For instance, you might become more self-critical or distrustful of your partner. So to help keep your growing self-awareness on a more positive course, you will want to develop self-compassion along with it.

With self-compassion you will be more inclined to view yourself and your partner in a realistic yet positive light; to trust that your partner will be there for you; and to feel good about your self-worth. For example, it can help you resist the tendency to view yourself as unlovable—even if your partner ends your relationship (it may be that she doesn't love you, but that's not the same as your being unlovable).

Psychologist Barbara Fredrickson's research on positive emotions (2001) suggests that the effects of self-compassion generate greater attachment-related security. Her research-based *broaden-and-build theory of positive emotions* basically states that positive emotions increase (or broaden) the pool of thoughts and actions that come to mind in any given circumstance. This helps people in the long term because these diverse options can be used as personal resources to be drawn on later. For instance, when children play, they are developing friendships, nurturing their creativity, and learning more about what makes people tick. This play puts them in a better position to cope with new situations or problems in the future. As an adult, your social-izing can help you to feel good about life and can provide connections to people who can be supportive, emotionally or pragmatically, if nec-essary. In these ways, positive emotions help you to develop the resources to be more resilient, to feel better about yourself, and to trust more in others.

In nurturing positive emotions, self-compassion opens people up to curiosity about, and desire for, even more positive experiences—including in their relationships. The good feelings also encourage people to search for positive meaning in their experiences, even the painful ones. All of this leads to growth.

For instance, consider Amy. Her preoccupied attachment style kept her feeling unworthy of love and unable to truly absorb the caring of others, leaving her less hopeful about finding a partner and stuck at home alone all too often. However, as she developed self-compassion, she could comfort herself as she struggled. This opened her up to doing more things that made her happy—such as socializing more with a few close friends, taking an online class, and even joining a singles hiking club. She met a man in the club who was also clearly uncomfortable in his own skin—something Amy could really sympa-thize with. She felt good about her ability to comfort this man, some-thing she could not have done if she had not experienced similar emotional struggles. *And* she recognized this as the beginning of a potential relationship!

In this chapter, I will discuss how you can actively nurture self-compassion by building your abilities in the aspects of self-compassion laid out by researcher Kristin Neff (2008): self-kindness, common humanity, and mindfulness (all discussed in chapter 5). I will begin with the latter two aspects, which propose a helpful attitude and per-spective that you can bring to your life. They can also, in turn, help you build up the first aspect, your self-kindness. As you will discover, these three areas overlap a lot and can often be thought of as different aspects of the same thing; so many of the exercises can fit into more than one category.

Common Humanity

One of the most painful emotions that a person can have is to feel disconnected and of little or no significant relevance to anyone else's life. If you struggle with attachment-related anxiety, you can probably relate to this (or the fear of this) all too well. Feeling like part of a greater humanity is a psychological lifeline that keeps people connected and gives them a sense of meaning. With it, they sense that they have value just for being. They can understand themselves and others because they are all cut from the same cloth, so to speak. If you doubt this applies to you or have difficulty really feeling it, then try the following exercises.

Exercises: Practice Generosity and Compassion

You can express and enhance your sense of common humanity by being generous and compassionate toward others. When you give from the heart, you are connecting with that other person's experience, while reinforcing the common sense of humanity between you. With this in mind, try one or both of these exercises:

Include kindness as part of your daily focus. It can be very helpful to make a commitment to act in a kind and generous way as part of your everyday activity. Choose to take the opportunities that arise for this. For instance, hold a door for someone or offer to help out a friend or neighbor.

Schedule kind and compassionate acts into your life. You might want to schedule volunteer activities. You can arrange to help out on a regular basis at a food pantry, school, or hospital. Check the Internet for other options—it's filled with opportunities to help others.

Offered with an open heart, such acts can provide you with a sense of meaning and a positive sense of yourself and others, as well as helping you to develop self-compassion.

♡

Exercise: Discover the Value in You

Believe it or not, you are a gem among gems. True, not all gems are the same. They differ in many ways, such as their color, durability, and shape—but they are all beautiful. They are often even loved when they're whole, uncut, and unpolished. And so it is with people. Though their characteristics differ, each and every one is precious—even you.

Not convinced? Think of it this way: Imagine entering a nursery filled with infants. They differ in size, coloring, facial characteristics, activity, and whether or not they have hair. They might be crying or feeding or just in the middle of their other important job—filling their diapers. Now look at each and every child. Which one is not precious? Ridiculous question, right? Given that they don't *do* anything of value, then their value must come from their very essence. And you, just like every other infant, came into this world with that same precious essence. It is a part of you—even if you have forgotten (or never learned) to recognize and tap into it.

Now imagine children on a playground. Just as with the infants, imagine pointing one out as not being precious or worthy of love. This just wouldn't feel right. Even if there were a child off to the side, perhaps shy or afraid, you would feel some sense of compassion for his struggle because you sense his value.

♡

Exercise: Be Your Own Best Friend

One good way to develop self-compassion is to leverage the compassion you already feel for others (especially loved ones in your life) and the common humanity between you. To begin, focus on a trait or experience that you have criticized yourself for. It may be something that has made you feel embarrassed, ashamed, different (and not in a good way), or "bad" in some other way. Now imagine that someone you care about is in the same situation. How would you feel toward that person? What would you think of him or her? Chances are that you would be more understanding and naturally compassionate.

While you cannot force yourself to have self-compassion, you *can* consciously think about how you would respond to others in your situation. If your reaction is to be compassionate, this might help you to question your self-criticism and consider being more compassionate toward yourself. The more you practice taking a self-compassionate perspective, the more familiar it will become—hopefully leading you to actually appreciate your thoughts, feelings, and actions, and to respond in a more self-compassionate way.

Mindfulness

As I explained in chapter 5, mindfulness is being conscious of your here-and-now experience with a full acceptance of it. Maintaining this perspective helps you to feel secure—much like the attuned and accepting parent helps his or her child to feel secure, especially in times of distress. And just as a secure child can metaphorically carry his emotionally available parent with him throughout life as a mental representation, mindfulness can help you provide this same kind of image for yourself. With it, painful emotions may still be painful, but you will be able to tolerate them better. You'll be less likely to compound your pain by fighting against them—getting angry with yourself for feeling upset, for example. Also, by watching your mind work, you'll gain a better understanding of yourself (which I discussed earlier as "mentalizing"). This will make you more open to self-compassion. So, as a mindful person, you will feel a greater sense of stability and insight about yourself, as well as a greater sense of happiness and well-being.

Mindfulness can benefit your relationship by helping you to respond in a more secure way to your partner. Rather than getting caught up in a chain reaction of thoughts and emotions related to your insecurities, you can stay grounded in the present while also being able to observe your experience with some perspective. As a result of this greater self-awareness, you'll be less likely to perceive a rejection from your partner (or potential partner) that isn't there—or to at least recognize when you are manufacturing it. You will also have more insight about your partner's experiences and motivations.

For instance, you might discover that your partner avoids asking you about your day because he fears that you will vent anger at him—not because he doesn't care. And you will be more likely to become tuned in to his real messages that you might not otherwise have been conscious of (particularly nonverbal ones, such as a look of concern as you walk in from work). By being aware and grounded in this way, you can truly "get"—not just intellectually understand—your partner or date, an essential step in developing intimacy.

Integrating Mindfulness into Your Life

If you wonder whether mindfulness and meditation really are helpful, rather than just a passing fad, you may find it convincing to learn that their benefits have been established by numerous scientific studies. According to an article in the American Psychological Association's professional magazine, *Monitor on Psychology* (Davis and Hayes, 2012), empirical research has shown that mindfulness can effectively reduce rumination, reduce stress, increase the ability to focus and suppress distractions, lessen emotional reactivity, increase cognitive flexibility (opening people to different ways of thinking about situations), enhance self-insight, increase compassion, and decrease psychological distress. While this can sound like a magical elixir peddled by some snake oil salesman, the research is all there to support the claims; and it's mounting steadily. If you are looking for a catch, it's this: mindfulness cannot be swallowed as a pill; it takes practice.

You can practice mindfulness—truly being in the here and now—by informally being mindful during your day. As Jon Kabat-Zinn (1994) suggests in his book *Wherever You Go, There You Are*, your mindfulness practice can be as simple as asking yourself at different times, "Am I awake now?" It can also be taking a moment to absorb your current experiences—thoughts, feelings, and sensations (for example, the smell of the room you are in, the feeling of your body on the chair—or, in my case right now, the sense of my fingers on the computer keyboard).

You can also choose to meditate: more formally setting aside time each day to practice mindfulness—it could be ten minutes, twenty minutes, an hour, or even longer, one or more times a day. Many people think that they can't meditate because they can't concentrate well or they get bored sitting still. However, this is based on a misunderstanding. You don't need a quiet mind, nor do you need to rein in your thoughts and force them to be still. Rather, mindfulness meditation involves paying attention to your experience, distractions and all. To maintain this perspective, rather than get pulled into the fray of their mind's activity, people begin with the practice of returning to some anchor, such as their breath.

The following exercises offer a way of learning some basics of mindfulness. The first two exercises introduce mindful breathing and mindfulness of other bodily sensations. Then a third exercise builds upon the first two, developing a mindful awareness of emotions. Later in this chapter, in the "Self-Kindness" section, a loving-kindness meditation exercise helps you to more directly nurture compassion.

Exercise: Breathing Mindfully

What can be more natural than breathing? Most of the time, it just happens. It happens while you are thinking and feeling and doing, and are generally distracted with the "contents" of your life. But if you get lost in all these activities, you can rely on your breath to be there as a neutral experience. It can help guide you back to the present moment and anchor you there.

To breathe mindfully, simply close your eyes or lower your gaze. Then shift your awareness to your breath. Follow the flow of your inhale through to its natural end. Note the pause at that point. Then follow your exhale to its end. There is no need to breathe more slowly or deeply, or to change your breath in any way. Simply keep your awareness on what your body is doing naturally. You might feel your chest or belly go up and down with each breath. On your inhale, you might notice a coolness in your nostrils or at the back of your throat. Whatever sensations you feel, just keep your awareness on them.

Maintaining awareness is simple, but not easy. Your mind will undoubtedly wander. The Buddhist description of this as "monkey mind" captures it well. Your mind is naturally restless and uncontrollable, jumping capriciously from one experience to the next. Once you see this activity, make note of it. Then choose to bring your awareness back to your breath. You might say something like, "I don't need to think about that right now. Instead, I want to return my awareness to my breath." Then gently do it.

Practice this each day by occasionally bringing your awareness to as few as one or two full breaths. Or you might decide to try it for a few minutes. You can also schedule one or two times daily to do it as a more formal meditation, sitting or lying in a comfortable position for fifteen or twenty minutes. Just as with exercising, it is important to start slowly and work up to your preferred practice—otherwise, you may find it too challenging and won't keep it up.

Exercise: Embodying Your Body

In addition to bringing mindfulness to your life through awareness of breath, you can bring yourself into the here and now by focusing on your bodily sensations. Choose a simple activity to be the object of your focus, such as showering, cutting vegetables, or walking. Then follow the directions below—paying close attention to the flow of your sensations.

For the purposes of this exercise, let's say you choose to walk mindfully, which is often done as a formal meditation. If you do this informally, a good time for it might be when walking from your car to your office, or while taking a stroll in your local park. However, you might find it easier to remain focused on your awareness of sensations when you are at home with no place to go and with no one watching—while say, walking back and forth, or in circles. Although you can do it at any pace, it can be helpful to walk very slowly (something that might make you self-conscious in public). Do this for ten minutes or longer—though there is no required length of time for this exercise, you will gain more if you challenge yourself in this way.

Orient yourself. Take a moment to bring your attention to your body, really feeling the position of it. Consciously let go of other concerns and acknowledge your intention to be mindful.

Focus awareness. Walk slowly enough that you can stay with every movement in your walking. Feel the muscles in your leg as you raise and then lower it. Attend to the soles of your feet as you gently put down your heel and then the rest of your foot. Feel how the weight of your body shifts onto that foot.

Note when you are distracted. When you become aware of being distracted by other thoughts, simply make that observation to yourself.

Gently refocus. Decide to let go of the distraction and return your attention to your sensations of walking.

As you do this exercise, keep in mind the marvel of being able to walk, of how your body is able to carry you. Be appreciative of being able to walk—something that not everyone can do.

♡

Exercise: Mindful Awareness of Emotions

Choose a time when you feel an emotion that is relatively mild in intensity. (You can later work up to meditating on stronger feelings.) Follow the steps below, but be aware that this is not a linear process with a finish line of being comfortably connected with your emotions. Instead, you might make progress one day or one moment, only to find yourself slipping back into more disconnection or distress at another time. Also, you might get a handle on emotions related to one area of your life, only to find yourself struggling more in another area. All of this is a natural part of life. But by learning to approach your emotions more mindfully, you will have a way to reconnect with them and to feel, once again, at home with them—and with yourself.

Anchor yourself in your breath. Given how easy it can be to get swept away in a wave of emotions or distressed thinking, it's important to know how to stay grounded and balanced. Meditating on your breath is a perfect way to do this. Your breath comes naturally, is life-sustaining and comforting, has its own rhythm that is easy to observe, and is always with you. So begin by doing the "Breathing Mindfully" exercise earlier in this chapter. Then remain seated with your eyes closed or lowered through the rest of this exercise.

Bring awareness to your body. Emotions are based in the body, so it is very helpful to connect with sensations in your body. Bring your awareness to the bottom of your feet, noting any sensations there. Then slowly bring your awareness up through your body to the top of your head. Make special note of any tension or unpleasant sensations. Rest your awareness there.

Identify your emotions. You may notice that particular emotions seem to emerge from, or be related to, these unpleasant sensations. If you can, label these emotions. This will help clarify your experience, but also give you some distance. Move your attention to an emotion that seems particularly strong. If it becomes too intense, return your awareness to your breath. Once you feel calmer, shift again to your sensations and emotions. Stay with them until you no longer feel distressed by them, or you feel you have done this enough. The goal is not to get rid of your feelings, but rather to experience them in an accepting way.

You might find it helpful to complete the "Identifying Your Emotions" exercise in chapter 6, either before doing this one or concurrently with it. You can also practice this during the day to help clarify distressing feelings and to loosen their grip on you.

Self-Kindness

As discussed in chapter 6, self-kindness means being kind to yourself. It means wanting to feel good in the moment, but also wanting what's best for yourself in the long run. It is an important motivation behind maintaining a healthy lifestyle. And it is essential to enabling you to offer yourself compassion when you are upset by your perceived inadequacies, mistakes, or failures.

Below are various ways in which you can express self-kindness. Some of them are proactively caring for yourself while others are more focused on offering yourself compassion when you struggle.

Stay Strong in Body

People who struggle with anxious attachment are often too quick to give up caring for themselves in favor of trying to earn the love of others by caring for them. While being nice to others is a positive quality, you hurt yourself when you don't keep up with taking care of your own body. So make it a priority to:

- Maintain a healthy diet.

- Get sufficient sleep.

- Exercise regularly.

By caring for yourself in these ways, you nurture the physical and emotional strength to enjoy life and face challenges effectively.

Feed Your Spirit

Research has supported the idea that it's important to nourish your connection to something larger than yourself, whether you call it God, nature, humanity, or anything else. This includes examining your fundamental values, considering what is most meaningful in your life, and finding a sense of awe in the world around you. It is often thought of as a search for the sacred—sometimes within the confines of religion and sometimes as part of a more personal journey.

Such a search can help you cope with the uncertainty and seeming randomness of life, providing a way of dealing with events beyond your control (for instance, work responsibilities prevent your boyfriend from meeting you for dinner) and with overwhelming events (a long-term girlfriend leaves you). It can also help you face your mortality.

You can nurture this aspect of your life in many ways, such as praying, meditating, attending religious services, studying religious texts, communing with nature, developing compassion and love, and doing good deeds. You might also nurture a sense that everything in the universe—including you—is interconnected, and so try to live in harmony with the universe.

Exercise: Find Healthy Ways to Comfort Yourself

Life can be hard. Really hard. And sometimes you just need some comfort. Unfortunately, too often people try to comfort themselves by relying on unhealthy behaviors, such as emotional eating, isolating, drinking, shopping, or gambling. To help guide you in a better direction, make a list of healthy ways to cope that at least sometimes work for you. For instance, you might include going for a walk, exercising at the gym, meeting with a friend, watching a movie, reading, praying, meditating, listening to music, or taking a bath. Place this list in an accessible place so that you can refer to it whenever you need to. But if you are really stuck in problematic ways of coping, seek professional help.

$\heartsuit$

Exercise: Practicing Gratitude

Research has shown that people are happier and more grateful after keeping a gratitude journal in which they write at least three things they are thankful for. Some research indicates you should do this daily, while other research suggests once a week is better. You need to find the frequency that is best for you.

A slight variation of this exercise is to focus on *qualities about you* that are positive. For instance, you might note that you improved your performance in some way at work, which highlights your caring, persistence, and effort there. Or you might focus on the fact that you were kind to an upset friend, or were sensitive enough to notice a beautiful sunset. This can help you develop more awareness, and eventual acceptance, of your positive attributes.

My personal experience with patients who have kept a gratitude journal is that they often followed a general pattern. They benefited from it most when they completed it daily for eight weeks. At first, they often had difficulty in even thinking of things to be grateful for. But then they transitioned to being able to do it more easily, but with conscious effort; to having it occur to them as they experienced things they were grateful for; and finally, to having gratitude be a part of them rather than something they had to try to do.

Exercise: Let Friends Warm Your Heart

Social connections are an important source of happiness, offering direct benefits that are also opportunities for personal growth.

Benefits From Having Friends	Personal Growth Opportunities
You can enjoy their company	…which gives you a sense of belonging.
They provide opportunities to learn about new things	…which nurtures your sense of curiosity, an important element in personal growth.

They offer chances to be kind or generous to others →	…which helps you see yourself positively and gain a sense of value.
You are exposed to people who think positively of you →	…which helps you to see yourself this way, too.
You are exposed to different perspectives on situations →	…which helps you develop empathy and compassion.
They are a resource for practical help →	…which offers you the chance to feel good about problem solving, in addition to enjoying direct benefits from the help.
They are a resource for emotional support →	…which may support you through difficult times, and help you experience your struggles as "part of being human" rather than feeling alone and different.

An easy way to begin developing friendships is to focus on people you have a shared interest with. Pursue your interests, getting involved in clubs, organizations, or classes. It's particularly helpful to find activities that give you an opportunity to see people on a regular basis. Then, show an interest in those people, or others around you. As a friendship develops, be open to doing things together and just having fun.

Focus the most energy on a few friends (maybe one to three people) who are good to you and seem to have your best interests in mind. As you feel emotionally safer with someone, share a bit more about yourself, including your feelings and thoughts. And really listen—so that you can get to know and connect with your friend. Also, listen *not just with your ears, but with your heart*—for how your friend feels about you. Pay attention to how her interest in, and acceptance of, you feels, how it seems to almost physically warm your heart.

If you tend to dismiss or minimize what you have to offer your friends, get out a sheet of paper and draw a line down the center of it. Then do the following:

Title the left side: "Friends." List your friends down the left side of the page. You can list anyone who seems to like you, from your dearest friend from childhood to a recent acquaintance.

Title the right side: "Valued Qualities in Me." Down this side of the page, list what you think these friends value in you. For each friend, ask yourself, "Why does he want to be my friend?" You might jot down words they might associate with you, such as caring, giving, honest, funny, enjoys the same activities, helpful, offers good advice, or good listener.

Consider your list of valued qualities. Read the qualities one at a time, letting them each sink in. Allow yourself to feel good about being valued and appreciated. If you find yourself minimizing or dismissing these things, that's okay. You may need time to adjust to them and accept them—much like how your eyes take time to adjust to seeing anything when you move from the darkness into the light. You might also find it helpful to practice seeing yourself through your friends' eyes.

Keep this list someplace easily accessible. Look it over frequently. Actively remind yourself that you *are* appreciated—that you are, in fact, worthy of love. Also, make sure to look at this list when you are feeling particularly vulnerable and flawed. At these times, you might even want to confide in one of the friends listed, with whom you feel emotionally safe.

♡

Exercise: Loving-Kindness Meditation

Your continued struggles cry out to be comforted by true love and acceptance. This reassurance is offered—at least somewhat—by loving-kindness meditations. Such meditations encourage you to see and feel the sense of personal worth that comes with secure attachment. They have also been shown to increase feelings of social connection (Hutcherson, Seppala, and Gross, 2008). With practice, you will be able to "feel the love."

In preparing for the following loving-kindness meditation, plan for a few minutes of undisturbed time. To help you gain a sense of mastery, it's best to start briefly, such as with ten minutes. Then you can work up to about twenty minutes. As you complete this meditation, approach it with a gentle, positive intention. Acknowledge distractions when they arise, then return your awareness to the exercise. If you have difficulty with the meditation, make note of this struggle and give yourself praise for working on this difficult task.

Sit down and settle into a comfortable position. Close or lower your eyes.

Bring your awareness to your breath. Follow the flow of your inhale and exhale for several breaths.

Bring your awareness to the heart area of your chest. Remind yourself that all people want to feel safe, happy, and at peace.

Repeat the following to yourself:

> May I feel safe.
>
> May I feel healthy.
>
> May I feel peaceful and happy.
>
> May I feel loved.

Recite each of these phrases slowly, allowing them to wash over you in a way that you can truly absorb. You might even want to repeat particular phrases or words to help you with this process. For instance, you might repeat the phrase "May I feel loved" several times slowly. Remember, this is a wish, not a command.

After you are able to connect with this meditation for yourself, you might want to offer it to others—family, friends, acquaintances, or even people you've never met. The more you practice this, the stronger your sense of compassion will grow.

If you have great difficulty in really feeling these loving wishes for yourself, consider first offering them to someone you already feel loving toward, such as a friend, a child, or a pet. Bring a clear image of that person (or animal) to mind so that you naturally feel a lightness. Now slowly recite the phrases for that person or animal.

May he feel safe.

May he feel healthy.

May he feel peaceful and happy.

May he feel loved.

After completing this heartfelt love offering, remind yourself that all people want these same feelings. Remind yourself that "all people" includes you. Now try the meditation with a focus on wishing these for yourself. If this proves too difficult, recognize and appreciate your efforts just the same.

Complete this meditation by returning awareness to your breath. Allow time to sit with the peaceful, positive feelings that accompanied the wishes of love and kindness.

♡

Compassionate Self-Awareness in a Nutshell

The practice of compassionate self-awareness is important for improving your romantic relationships and feeling better about yourself. Though developing this is a challenging process, the variety of exercises in chapters 6 and 7 offer specific ways to increase your self-awareness and self-compassion. Use your uplifting dreams for the future, as well as the pains of your present and past relationships, to motivate you to persist in your efforts. Return, as needed, to the exercises you think will help at any particular time. Along the way, you will have moments of insight, and you'll experience times when you make better choices that enable you to enjoy more moments of happiness in your life and relationships. Take the time to appreciate these. Remember that a fulfilling life is one that you appreciate in the moment, even as you continue toward a better future.

PART FOUR

Lighting Up Your Love Life

Chapter 8

Finding Someone Who Will Accept You and Warm Your Heart

Finding that special someone can seem straightforward—*Funny, romantic, fit man seeks same qualities in a woman for a lifetime of friendship and love.* But it rarely is—after meeting this Prince Charming, you might wonder about his definition of "fit" or "romantic" or even "funny." But even more problematic than other people's baggage is your own—as I've detailed in earlier chapters.

However, you don't need to remain stuck in these dilemmas. Instead, as you develop compassionate self-awareness, you'll find that you are in a better position to find someone who is a good fit for you—not an objectively perfect mate, but a person who can accept and love you for who you really are, be emotionally available to you, and can warm your heart. And just as importantly, it can help you to walk away from bad situations. It makes this possible by helping you to clearly see what you are looking for in a relationship and follow through on that vision.

Set a Goal for a Healthy Relationship

To succeed in relationships, as in any aspect of life, you must know what it is you want. While you might stumble upon a good relationship out of dumb luck, it helps to be clear about your goal. You can use this clarity to point you in the generally correct direction and to guide you along the way.

In broad terms, what makes for a secure attachment in childhood also makes for a secure relationship in adulthood. So you can think about relationships as having the following three basic characteristics:

Emotional availability: Children need their parents physically and emotionally close to help them feel secure, but adult relationships are more dependent on the partners being emotionally close. While separations and long-distance romantic relationships can cause a strain, they are not necessarily deal-breakers. However, partners must accept and be responsive to each other's needs. When your partner remains emotionally distant or hostile, you will probably feel alone, rejected, or abandoned, and may question your value as a person.

Safe haven: Just as a child runs back to his mother when threatened or upset, partners in a healthy relationship turn to each other when they need reassurance or support during difficult times. Because life always includes at least some pain and tiring obstacles, it's important to have a partner who can offer comfort, help, and respite from those difficulties. People who know they have this trusted "port in a storm" are less overwhelmed by life's challenges. Unfortunately, if your partner is dismissing or critical, then you won't turn to him; or if you do turn to him, you will ultimately feel rejected.

Secure base: To feel fulfilled in life and truly loved in a relationship, it's important for people to be able to pursue their heart's desires—or even simply to be able to explore what those desires may be. Healthy relationships are ones in which partners encourage and support those efforts.

As you think about these qualities of a healthy relationship, remember that both partners need to work together to create them. Partners need to be open to accepting and being accepted, which is essential to emotional availability; to comforting and being comforted, ensuring a safe haven in times of trouble; and to encouraging and being encouraged, making the relationship a secure base from which to explore the world. Although you are probably more concerned about a partner being able to offer these "gifts" to you, it is equally important for him to be able to receive them, because an open give-and-take dynamic nurtures relationships. Similarly, it is essential that you are capable of offering and receiving these things.

While these remarks provide a sense of what you want to aspire to, they are short on details for how to pick a partner who is good for you and how to proceed from there. For guidance on this, read on.

What to Look for in a Partner

A good partner can help you become more of the person you want to be. Researchers Drigotas, Rusbult, Wieselquist, and Whitton (1999) identified and found support for this process, which they termed the *Michelangelo phenomenon*. Much like Michelangelo would, through sculpting, bring out the beautiful forms that he could see in a block of stone before him, a loving partner can bring out your optimum or "ideal" self and reveal this beautiful nature in you.

Theoretically speaking, the person best able to be there for you in this way has the attributes listed below. I offer this with the qualification that your needs might be met by someone whose traits don't match parts of this list. That's okay. This is only meant as a rough guideline—as something to consider (though to seriously consider) as you look for a potential partner or evaluate how well the person beside you is meeting your needs. With that in mind, you want a partner who is:

Securely attached and mature. Because such people are comfortable with themselves and their connections, they are capable of being emotionally close, as well as wanting themselves and their partners to explore separate, personal interests. They are also able to reflect on themselves and their lives in an open, insightful, and emotionally connected way. This enables them to acknowledge their limitations and nondefensively admit to their mistakes—all without sacrificing a positive sense of themselves. Understanding that others are similarly flawed, they are able to readily forgive their partners.

An effective communicator. Such partners are good at listening and sharing, which helps them to nurture and maintain close relationships. They can also effectively work through disagreements. In part, they have these strengths because they are generally good at identifying and managing their emotions—a definite plus as you try to connect with another person and work through the difficulties that will inevitably arise in an emotionally intimate relationship.

Appreciative of you. It is not enough to fall in love. Because relationships are cocreated, they will make you happy in the long term only if your partner respects and values you—and works to express this in some way. Your partner must show an interest in getting to know you. And, although it's a steep learning curve at first, the quest to know you better should never totally plateau. You will also be happiest and reach your greatest potential with support and encouragement to explore your personal interests.

A good fit. It is important to enjoy spending time together. This generally means having at least some shared interests. But it definitely means enjoying activities together, even if that just involves having engaging conversations. Sharing, or at least respecting, each other's values is very important for a long-term relationship. And the more those values affect daily life, the more important it is for them to be shared. For instance, disaster awaits when one partner is determined to have children and the other partner is absolutely against it. Or if one partner is committed to a nomadic lifestyle—say, a career as a traveling salesperson—the relationship will work much better if the other partner is supportive of that.

Ready for a relationship. Your partner must be willing to make the relationship a priority. This means devoting time and giving attention to it, both when you are physically together and when you are apart. It also involves viewing sex and emotional closeness as two aspects of an intimate relationship that support each other. Finally, a potentially good partner will believe that you—as a couple—are responsible for each other's happiness.

Again, it's important to remember that you do not need to find Mr. or Ms. Perfect—which is good, because neither of those people exist. And you don't even have to find Mr. or Ms. Perfect-For-Me. That can prove to be an unending search with the constant hope of finding a better person just around the corner. Rather, what you need to find is Mr. or Ms. Good-For-Me. I am not suggesting that you settle for someone you are not really happy with, but rather that you make sure you have your priorities straight. With that solid foundation, you'll be able to accept a little messiness, or no interest in climbing a corporate ladder, or some other "fault" much more easily—and maybe you can even come to appreciate it. For instance, less-than-ambitious career aspirations might be a reflection of the value your partner places on relationships and other nonmaterial aspects of life.

One final caution: Don't be too quick to move past a "nice-but-boring" date. As Levine and Heller (2010) note, sometimes people equate their attachment-related anxiety with the feeling of being in love. When someone is comfortable to be with and seems accepting of you, your attachment-related anxiety might not be triggered. So it's entirely possible that the "nice person" you met might be a great fit for you—despite the lack of immediate "excitement."

Exercise: Imagining Your Perfect Partner

Imagine walking along in some isolated area; you come upon an old wedding ring half stuck in the ground. As you pick it up and wipe off the dirt to see the design on it, out comes a genie. He has the very special power of being able to conjure up the partner of your dreams, or else to change your imperfect partner into that ideal. All he needs is your wish list for what you want in a partner. Think carefully before answering— your future depends on it.

To help with this task, make a written list. Include all the qualities you can think of—personality, way of relating to others, way of relating to you, information regarding parenting (for instance, desire to be a parent, number of children desired, or beliefs about each parent's role), occupation, physical characteristics, lifestyle, priorities, and interests. Include your idea of how the two of you would enjoy spending time together.

The more detail you provide, the better. Of course, there is no genie (sorry!), and you will probably never meet anyone who fits everything on your list. But by doing this exercise, you will have a better chance of recognizing whether or not someone is a good fit.

♡

Exercise: Imagining Your Perfect Relationship

The "right" partner can help you nurture greater security in yourself and your relationship, and also help you develop better relationship skills. But even if you could "order up" that person, doing so would not be enough to ensure a happy future together. You must also be part of creating it. So think about what assets you have that nurture a healthy relationship, and ways that you might change and grow—with the support of a good partner—to be better at nurturing one. As you do, remember that developing such a relationship will take time—both because developing intimacy takes time and because you will not be instantly cured of your insecurities. To help you think this through, consider these questions:

- How will it affect you to have a caring, attentive, faithful partner?

- How do you think this relationship will feel different for you, compared to what you felt in previous ones?

- What will be the *first signs*, both in your interactions and in how you feel, that it is better than previous relationships?

- What other small and big signs will you see along the way?

- As your attachment-related anxiety lessens, what will you do more of in this relationship? How will this be different from what you did in your previous ones?

- As your attachment-related anxiety lessens, what will you do less of in this relationship? How will this be different from what you did in your previous ones?

- In what ways will this partner and relationship help you to manage your attachment-related anxiety better?

- How do you imagine this new behavior on your part will feel different for this partner (as compared to what your previous partners likely felt in response to your old behaviors)?

- What will ultimately be different in this healthier relationship that is less burdened by your attachment-related anxiety?

- How will this relationship help you to maintain your newly found security?

Now, *slowly* read over all that you've written. Then reread it. Imagine it. Give it a chance to seep in. Allow yourself to have a sense of really experiencing it. Getting to know what this looks and feels like will help you know and feel in your heart what it is that you are really seeking.

Panning for Gold

Even with guidelines for what to look for in a partner, you might wonder, *How will I know when I've found someone who is just right for me?* It's tempting to say that you'll know her when you meet her. But that implies that you'll experience something unmistakably distinctive, like hearing angels sing. This is *not* something you can rely on because people are often deceived by their biases.

Your struggles with questioning your importance to others or your worthiness of love can affect your relationships and choice of partner in a number of ways. For instance, it can put you at risk of not recognizing when close is too close. Your desire to have a partner or potential partner right there with you much of the time (as reassurance of his love) might make him feel uncomfortable, stifled, or controlled—especially if he is not feeling that same urge for closeness. Even if his need for closeness does match yours, consider whether you are feeling supported and encouraged in developing your separate interests—or whether you are giving up those aspects of yourself in exchange for the connection. You might also find that your insecurities prevent you from walking away when your partner is rejecting or overly distant. These are the kinds of situations that cause people to feel that they've "given up their power" or "lost" themselves in their relationships.

If you are someone who is more focused on your independence and the things you do than on emotional connections, your loneliness might be confusing—though it might also help motivate you to find a partner. You might choose someone who is similarly self-sufficient, but this will likely leave you feeling all the more alone; your respect for her self-sufficiency is not enough. On the other hand, choosing someone who is more interested in a deep emotional connection might leave you feeling uncomfortably close, and possibly critical of her neediness.

Fortunately, there is a way through this confusing mess, and it's with compassionate self-awareness as your guide. By being compassionately in touch with your thoughts and emotions, and being able to reflect on the reasons for your inner experiences and behaviors—mentalizing—you are in a better position to separate potentially good partners from those who will cause you recurring distress. So think back to the insights about yourself that you've gained so far in this book. If you need to, review the exercises from chapters 5 and 6 to hone your compassionate self-awareness.

With that perspective, look again at the exercises you've completed in this chapter about finding your "ideal" partner. This approach will help you a lot as you consider whether a particular person is right for you.

At some point, you might feel passionately about a new person and be almost uncontrollably driven to want to get close fast. But if this has been a pattern, slow down! Take note that diving in so quickly has not produced the long-term, healthy, happy relationship you want. It's not that whirlwind romances never work out, but you increase your chances of success by giving yourself time—time to get to know the other person, and for the other person to get to know you.

No matter how well you click or how much you feel like you've "known each other forever," true intimacy can never happen all at once. Remind yourself regularly that there is so much you *don't* know about each other. To strengthen your patience, turn to other sources of support in your life—such as family, friends, and fulfilling and validating activities. Also, return to the self-kindness exercises in chapter 7 to help you. With a sense of acceptance and value in other areas of your life, you can lessen the pressing need to create an instant, perfect (so-you-won't-be-rejected) love.

The process of trying to find a good partner is a lot like panning for gold. It can be exciting when you find something that sparkles. But you need to be cautious. If you mistake fool's gold for the real thing, you will eventually find yourself alone and distraught. And in the meantime, you will have lost opportunities to find the real thing, and might become jaded about the possibility of ever having this kind of "wealth." So learn to recognize and toss out any fool's gold. Then you'll be more assured that when you find love, it's the real thing!

Be on the Alert for a Pursuit-Withdrawal Relationship

As I discussed in chapter 3, getting caught in a pattern of pursuit-withdrawal with an avoidant person is a common problem. And relationships defined by this dynamic are unlikely to leave you feeling happy, truly supported, or fulfilled. So pay close attention when you meet someone who:

- Displays an interest in you

BUT

- Does not seem to care about or attend to your feelings;

- Does not respect or want to hear about your thoughts or interests; or

- Dismisses your desire for closeness as being too needy.

Your gut might churn from the conflicting messages. This person offers hope of your *finally* being loved, but also supports your belief that you lack value or are unworthy of love. In response, you might feel compelled to try harder to earn the love and acceptance that you seek. But your efforts probably won't work. The extra excitement that you feel is most likely not so much the happiness of having met your true love as it is anxiety about being rejected. And the other person's need for distance will continue to leave you feeling rejected.

However, if you think there really is hope, talk directly with your partner about what you are thinking, feeling, and looking for. He might be willing to work with you on improving the relationship. You might also find that the problem lies more in your insecurities than in your partner's behavior—in which case you need to focus on working through your issues. Go back to the exercises on developing compassionate self-awareness to help you with this. You can even enlist your partner's support. In the end, though, transforming a relationship always takes two. If your partner won't work with you (no matter who is responsible for which problems), I suggest that you try couples therapy. If that doesn't work, you should seriously consider ending the relationship.

Exercise: Resisting the Pull of a Pursuit-Withdrawal Relationship

Even with good self-awareness, it can be very hard to leave and stay away from a destructive pursuit-withdrawal dynamic. People often feel a strong pull to prove their worth by continuing to try to make the relationship work. Or if they do walk away, they often feel the need to patch things up soon afterward, even if they don't genuinely believe their partners have changed. When successfully reunited, they feel a relief-laced enthrallment of being loved by their partners again. But their struggles with feeling abandoned, rejected, or alone usually resume before too long.

So, if you decide that ending a pursuit-withdrawal relationship (whether it's new or established) is the best course of action, you can help yourself a lot by developing a plan and making efforts that are informed by self-compassion.

Look critically at the relationship. When your resolve to end the relationship or stay away from it weakens, remind yourself of your partner's pattern of distancing. It will help you see that your partner is not really available for a close relationship. This is not a matter of your value, but rather of his issues. Think about it: Isn't this what you would believe and tell a good friend in the same situation?

Remind yourself of how the relationship makes you feel. Although being apart is painful after a breakup, it can help to remember that being together was painful, too. What hurts isn't so much suffering the loss of love, but suffering the loss of the *fantasy* of having your partner emotionally there, supportive, and accepting of you. Remind yourself that your pain is understandable, but returning to your former partner will not alleviate it. In the long run, the only way to do this is to stay away.

Also, in the "Moving On" section of chapter 10 you will find two exercises that deal with this issue: "Is It Worth It?" and "Letting Go." These will help you gain clarity on your decision to end your relationship and provide guidance on how to follow through with that decision.

$\heartsuit$

Spin a Supportive Web

Imagine a spider web. Note that it is held up by many threads. If you cut one, the web still stays in place. However, if the spider dangles from one thread and you cut it, the spider will naturally fall. Similar to a spider, you are supported better by many social connections.

Of course, your social network is much more complicated than a spider's web. However, it is still true that you will be better off by having a number of "threads" to support you in life. If you are essentially relying on just one person or trying to find the one person who will make you feel valued and appreciated, you will cling to that person for dear life. This desperate need works against your developing the sense of security necessary for any healthy relationship.

To take this metaphor a step further: A spider builds a web not just as a safe place to reside, but also as a tool in feeding itself. Similarly, healthy relationships serve functions beyond just providing a comfort zone. They are a source of fun and enjoyment and sexual pleasure, and are also a secure base to support you in pursuing your interests. But if all you can focus on is getting reassurance, then your anxiety about this can interfere with meeting these needs. For instance, you might not be able to appreciate purely fun experiences. Or you might so much want to be valued that you perceive greater connection or interest from someone else than is really there—and rely heavily on it.

To avoid this emotionally precarious situation, it is extremely helpful to support yourself with many threads. Develop relationships with family, friends, and neighbors—from acquaintances to close connections. Invest yourself in work or hobbies or volunteering. Create a life where there are many people and activities "holding you up"—each one providing you with some sense of being valued and appreciated.

Some people keep themselves from getting focused too soon on one person by dating more than one at a time. By having a sense that there are many potential partners out there, you will feel emotionally freer to take your time in deciding on one person. If you are open to "just dating," you have the luxury of time in deciding whether any particular relationship holds real promise. If this sounds appealing, great! Go for it. If not, that's okay, too. However, you still need to actively pursue dating. Although your dream date might just stumble into your life, this is much more likely to happen if you are out there where that special someone can trip over you.

Once you are in a romantic relationship, you will be more prepared to nurture it if you already feel fulfilled and valued in other areas of your life. Your partner will hopefully still be your main go-to person for comfort and support (your main attachment figure), but the relationship will not be overtaxed. You'll approach it with a sense of feeling secure—enjoying emotional closeness, supporting your partner's individual interests, expecting your partner to support your interests, having fun together, and appreciating sexual intimacy.

Chapter 9

Nurturing a Relationship You Feel Secure In

Watching couples dance together can be totally engaging. It's fascinating to watch two people flow together in perfectly timed movements. Those who are most successful seem to be connected by some magnetic force. Seeing them dance gives the vicarious experience of enjoying a perfect connection with someone else. What can be more enticing than that?

After finding a romantic partner, you'll want to nurture a relationship that at its best can feel like that perfectly coordinated dance. In such a relationship, the two of you would work well together, communicate effectively, and trust each other, all the while being in tune with yourselves as well as each other. Even at its worst, you'd still want it to be a coordinated effort. You'd find ways to accept and work with differences between you, rather than trying to force each other to change.

Part of the beauty of enjoying such a supportive relationship is that it helps you to feel more secure within yourself, as well as within your relationship. Also, as you may remember from chapter 2, you can even "earn" a secure attachment style in adulthood by developing compassionate self-awareness and enjoying a relationship with an emotionally available and supportive attachment figure. So, it is well worth the effort to do your part in nurturing a healthy, mutually supportive relationship.

Self-Disclosure

Your first interactions with a potential partner set the stage for how the story of your relationship will unfold. In the very beginning, it will go most smoothly if the two of you open up to each other in synchrony. One of you shares something personal and the other one responds with understanding, compassion, and a similar kind of disclosure. You both feel closer, which encourages you to share more, deepening your level of openness. As you enjoy these intimate moments, you also develop a sense of safety and trust in each other's company. The fondness and affection that inevitably develop from these interactions are essential in maintaining a happy long-term relationship.

Getting to know each other with this kind of give-and-take probably won't go smoothly if you have an insecure attachment style. For instance, you might hope that sharing many of your struggles right away will win the attention, comfort, and reassurance of your partner. On the other hand, your need for closeness might make you feel too vulnerable to share; so, instead, you might remain distant and closed off. In both cases, you risk turning off your partner. Also, because your focus is on how your partner can help or hurt *you*, it interferes with getting to know her and having empathy for her.

If the way you tend to share has derailed your relationships, then it's time to approach it differently. Begin by thinking about your motivations for disclosing—or not disclosing. If you have trouble identifying these, review the exercises in chapter 6 ("Developing Self-Awareness"). Then, as you go forward, pay attention to when and how you share.

If you tend to feel compelled to escape loneliness by getting close fast, pull back a bit. Reach out to old friends, as well as new, developing friendships. You might also want to become involved in activities that offer a sense of being part of something bigger than yourself, which can lessen your sense of being separate and lonely. For instance, you might engage in church or temple activities or even just create a photo album for a family member. You can help out a charity by entering a bike-a-thon; or volunteer your time for organizations such as Habitat for Humanity or Literacy Volunteers of America. You can also allow yourself to connect consciously with the lonely feelings and respond by comforting yourself rather than rushing to have someone else comfort you.

You might, at the right time, want to share your personal struggles with your partner as a way to get closer and help her understand you. But tempting as it might be to "unpack all your baggage" and share each and every item in detail, be judicious about what you share. Generally speaking, share enough for your partner to understand so that she can be empathic and supportive. The rest can come out, if you so choose, with time.

For instance, you might disclose, "I feel nervous about letting my guard down because my last girlfriend criticized me all the time." By choosing not to say more about it for the moment, you can keep your attention on your current relationship. You give this prospective girl-friend a chance to share about herself or ask more about you. She might say, "I know just how you feel...." Or, on the other hand, she might prompt you with, "What do you mean?" In this way, you can guide your disclosures and emerging sense of connection to happen in synchrony with your partner—leading to a sense of warmth and affection that can hopefully bind you through the years.

Interdependence: Being One "Whole Half"

It's important to develop a connection in which you and your partner are not separate from each other or dependent on each other; rather, you're interdependent. In interdependence, you rely on each other for comfort and encouragement while still feeling like whole people who are able to function independently.

To be interdependent you must gauge your partner's needs for closeness and autonomy, as well as your own. When either of you feels that these needs are not being met—as will definitely happen at times—it is vital that you communicate effectively to fix the problem. Because such communication involves making yourself vulnerable, you have to believe that it's possible for you and your partner to work through issues. This perspective is freeing because you won't experience every problem as an omen that your relationship is going to end soon. You can be patient as you naturally get closer, no longer feeling a need to rush intimacy. You also won't feel compelled to give up—saving yourself from "inevitable" hurt—just because things aren't going smoothly. Instead, when you work with your partner to meet each of your needs for closeness and autonomy, you become a team, held together by love, trust, and emotional availability to each other. At your best, you can be like those amazing dancing couples that move so beautifully in synchrony.

Of course, if you deeply fear rejection, the natural fluctuations in closeness and autonomy that happen in relationships can be a serious problem. You may feel great when you and your partner are close (such as when you're cuddling up together watching a movie), but you'll probably also be extremely upset with every instance of increased distance (such as when your partner is preoccupied or withdrawn). This kind of emotional roller-coaster ride can take its toll on any relationship.

You can minimize these problems by picking a partner who is truly emotionally available and capable of working with you on balancing intimacy and autonomy, as well as other issues. With such a person, you are also likely to feel more secure, comfortable, and motivated to pursue your own interests, as well as feeling more comfortable with him pursuing his own interests.

Exercise: Improving Your Dance of Intimacy

This exercise can help you learn to manage closeness and autonomy better. It guides you to make note of the benefits of the one of those two you tend to shy away from, and to take action on your observations. Before you begin, you might find it helpful to look back at the chapter 2 exercise "How Well Do You Balance Autonomy and Closeness?" Reviewing that previous exercise can clarify the balance that you tend to look for in a relationship or currently have in your relationship.

Keep in mind that there is not some magical, fixed ratio of autonomy to intimacy that makes for a healthy relationship. People tend to have different needs, and these needs are often in flux. Relationships do best when partners' needs are basically in sync with each other on a general level, and yet the partners are also able to accommodate each other at any particular moment.

Challenge Your Craving for Intimacy

If you feel strongly compelled to be close with your partner while minimizing differences between you, allow yourself to play devil's advocate. Think about activities you might enjoy pursuing without your partner. These can be anything. For instance, you might want to take a class, start your own garden, or go out weekly with friends. Imagine how freeing or energizing it might be to do these things. If you are aware of also feeling anxious, remember that this is just a thought experiment. You are only making a list; you don't have to do anything you don't want to.

To work through your anxiety or uncertainty, you might find it helpful to talk with supportive people in your life or to journal about your thoughts. You can also complete some of the self-awareness exercises in chapter 6 or the self-compassion exercises in chapter 7.

When you are ready, talk with your partner. Pay attention to how he responds to the idea of your doing more on your own. If he is supportive, run with it and report back to him how it's working for you to pursue your interests—and how much you appreciate his support. If he is at all hesitant, encourage him to share why and discuss the pros and cons of your pursuing your interests. If his concerns seem reasonable, then talk together about what you can do that you are both comfortable with.

Also, remember that this is a two-way street. Ask him about his interests and listen for how it would feel for him to pursue them—or, if he's already doing that, how it already does make him feel. Think about what it would be like to support your partner in pursuing his interests. For instance, he might like looking at antique cars. Imagine how it would feel to see him excitedly telling you about some cars he's seen or read about. Allow yourself to feel your partner's appreciation for having you to share this with.

Challenge Your Need to Be Self-Reliant

For you, being emotionally open and vulnerable might feel threatening—or just unnecessary. But if you feel lonely, you are suffering from a lack of closeness. If you take the chance of opening up more, you will probably find that you enjoy the closeness this typically brings. On the other hand, thinking about disclosing your experiences might make you feel uncomfortable or anxious. Just keep in mind that you don't have to do anything now. You are just thinking about it.

If you have trouble connecting with—or being clear about—your emotions, return to chapter 6's self-awareness exercises. If the idea of making yourself vulnerable stops you in your tracks, review the self-compassion exercises in chapter 7. It can help to remember that this is a process. It takes time.

When you are ready, talk with your partner. Likewise, when she shares, take a curious stance with her. Ask for more information about what she thinks, feels, or has experienced. The idea is to engage more and to get to know yourself and your partner as well as you possibly can. This kind of open conversation can help to close the gap between you, easing your sense of feeling alone or lonely.

Whether you are working to increase autonomy or intimacy (or to become more flexible in accommodating changing needs in yourself and your partner), you will find that your efforts can pay off with a happier relationship. You'll probably feel more understood, valued, supported, and connected. You might even feel an increased desire for, and appreciation of, physical intimacy. In addition, you'll probably also notice that some issues will disappear, or at least become much more minimal. For instance, you might notice that you are no longer so susceptible to loneliness, boredom, restlessness, jealousy, or general distrust—and that you are less inclined to fear rejection or to feel an existential sense of being alone in the world.

♡

Keeping Your Connection Going

Too often, people let the stresses of daily life bump their relationships to the bottom of the priority list. They lose a sense of closeness with their partners, to the point that each basically leads separate lives. As someone with attachment-related anxiety, you have the advantage of essentially having an early warning system for this. As the two of you begin to drift apart, it will hurt—and this can prompt you to reach out to your partner. If your partner doesn't seem as bothered by the distance, it's important to know that he is nevertheless probably feeling the loss of connection on some level, or *will* feel it if the pattern continues. Hopefully, with encouragement from you, the two of you can work to become closer again.

To close the gap that exists (or prevent the distance from growing), it is essential that you and your partner do the daily "work" of relationships to connect, support each other, and enjoy each other's company. You can do this in three basic ways:

Touch base daily. This means that you must talk daily about what's happened earlier that day or what your plans are for the next day. These conversations will help you stay in sync and provide a chance for you to support each other through both difficult and exciting times. Your conversation could be as short as ten minutes, but it is still important.

If you tend not to pursue interests separately from your partner, these conversations can be a way for your partner to support and encourage you in expanding your horizons. Pursuing your own interests can give you a chance to feel excited and fulfilled, and can serve as an opportunity to bring this positive energy into the relationship.

Spend quality time together. Without shared experiences, there isn't much of a relationship. This might seem obvious, but again, couples frequently get caught up in their activities apart from each other. So make plans each week to go out for dinner or to a festival, or just to take walks and chat.

Combine forces on a shared project. Often couples find that this also helps to unite them. In many cases, the biggest shared project is that of raising children. However, you can also work together on other goals, such as decorating your home or investing yourselves in a worthy cause.

Accentuate the Positive

Love isn't just how you feel; it is the act of showing that you care about your partner for your partner's sake. And for your relationship to succeed in the long term, you must love *and* be loved. This means that you and your partner must act in ways that help you both to feel valued, cared about, and wanted.

To create such a loving connection, do what you can to accentuate the positive in your partner and your relationship. Consider this a guiding principle in maintaining a happy relationship. As you will see in the following exercises, there are many little ways that you can do this every day. The better you are at making these behaviors a regular part of your lives, the happier you will be as a couple.

Exercise: Heighten Your Attraction with Activity

Sexual attraction is essential in keeping your romance alive, whether you are with a prospective partner or in an established relationship. And this attraction is intensified by physical arousal. Research has shown that physical arousal can be generated by any source, from exercising to experiencing intense emotions, such as anger, sadness, and excitement (Pines, 2005). But your mood also influences attraction: you are more likely to feel attracted to someone and to express this when you are in a good mood rather than in a bad one.

If attachment-related anxiety has generally driven your attraction, then it is particularly important to find other, healthier ways to excite sexual attraction and enhance romantic interest. What follow are some suggestions for activities to do alone before your date or with your partner—though you might want to think of your own ideas.

- Bicycling

- Hiking

- Rollerblading

- Playing tennis

- Brisk walks

- Dancing

- Going to concerts

- Watching emotionally charged movies—say action, comedy, or romance

- Traveling to new places

Engaging in these physically arousing and fun experiences can open up a whole new world for you. Rather than relying on your fear of rejection to fan the flames of your passion, you can feel attracted to someone who also helps you to feel emotionally safe.

♡

Exercise: Show Your Love

One of the best ways to express your love is to show it with physical affection. You can do this in countless ways. You might hold hands, hug, offer a shoulder or foot massage, or even just quickly and gently touch your partner's back. And, of course, there's making love.

Equally important to touching your partner is really taking in when your partner touches you. A sure way to feel loved is to soften and absorb that touch. If you are distracted by thinking about other things or minimize the touch by thinking it doesn't mean anything, then you are, in that moment, failing to take in your partner's love. So pay attention.

Touch comes more easily to some people than others. If you and your partner tend not to be physically affectionate, then you might want to work on touching more—and maybe even get your partner to join you. Many people make it a part of their routine to hug each morning or evening. (I'm talking about an extended taking-each-other-in hug, not a quick clench-and-release.) You and your partner might try that or try giving each other back or foot massages. You might also begin just by cuddling while watching TV. It's okay if this feels awkward at first. With practice, you will find that the discomfort lessens and is replaced by a feeling of comfort and warmth.

♡

Exercise: Make Compliments a Habit

Just as physical contact can strengthen your relationship, so too can words. They can be expressed in powerfully touching ways. For instance, there was the wonderful moment in the movie *As Good as It Gets* (1997) when obsessive-compulsive, misanthropic, and generally off-putting Melvin (Jack Nicholson) says to Carol (Helen Hunt), "You make me want to be a better man."

Your compliments don't always have to be that dramatic. Often, the best compliments are simple observations that express appreciation for your partner. You might let your partner know that he is a wonderful cook or that she is a patient mother. Then there is always the heartfelt "I love you." When you share these positive sentiments on a regular basis, you both can't help but feel better for it.

So, if your relationship is short on compliments, change that. Make it a habit to compliment your partner at least once every day. And if your partner is also short on compliments, talk with her about this. You might even ask her to read this section. Then make a pact for both of you to compliment each other one time each day for a week. Check in at the end of that week to see how it went. Let each other know how being complimented felt. (That's also a good thing to do right after you receive a compliment.) Then you might want to recommit to another week. Keep doing this—making a commitment to compliment each other daily for some specified length of time and then checking in afterward. Repeating this exercise will help turn it into a habit that you actively encourage together.

♡

Exercise: Loving Actions

Doing nice things for each other often comes naturally during the beginning of a relationship. He buys you flowers. You send him a thoughtful text. You both recognize and celebrate special occasions, such as birthdays or significant accomplishments. Often, however, relationships go through periods of time when partners take each other for granted and don't put much effort into caring for each other. During these times, partners feel disconnected and alone, or even rejected.

If you are in a new relationship and your partner is not displaying caring actions (or is very inconsistent in doing so), then you would be wise to at least question whether he is the right person for you. Ask yourself whether the electricity you feel is really more anxiety about, or fear of, rejection, and whether your partner's attachment style is triggering this. Review the "Panning for Gold" section in chapter 8, which addresses pursuit-withdrawal relationships.

It's important that you *and* your partner make conscious efforts to do things that say you care and want to make the other happy. However, you may not really know what would, or does, make your partner happy, and the same could be true for him. This possibility is uncomfortable for many people. They believe that their partner should know what makes them happy without being told, and that telling their partner what they like invalidates the action itself. However, it's unfair to expect others—even those who love you—to read your mind. Also, to be upset about this is to miss the point that when your partner wants to hear what makes you happy and then acts on it, it says something positive about him. Really, explicitly stating what you want is a no-lose proposition.

So, with this in mind, read the following exercise on asking for what you want. If you feel ready to tackle it, ask your partner to read it, too, or explain it to him. If either of you is hesitant about doing this, take the time to think and talk about what makes you hesitant. For instance, some people feel that sharing what they want opens them up to being rejected, or might make them seem needy. Hopefully, by talking openly you can reassure each other that you simply want to make each other happy. After you've talked, you might feel ready to work on the exercise as it is written; or you might choose to simplify it, as I will explain in the first step.

Make a list of actions your partner could take that would make you feel loved. This could be something that he already does or used to do, or something that you'd like him to do. Be concrete. For instance, you might write: bring me water for my nightstand every evening, hold my hand when we walk together, tell me you love me, sit next to me when we watch TV, or accompany me to a basketball game. Steer clear of asking for something that has been the source of conflicts or tension. Also, do not share this list with each other yet.

If you want to begin a bit more slowly, each of you can pick just two actions that you would like the other to do. Pick ones that you think would be acceptable—maybe something that your partner used to do or has offered to do on occasion. Later, after you have experienced positive results, you can move to doing this exercise in its full form.

Talk about what it would be like to share your lists. Share both positive and negative feelings. You might begin by saying that you are looking forward to hearing his requests. But you might also share that you are uncomfortable with the exercise. Perhaps you fear sounding demanding or having him reject everything you ask for. As you talk, it is the job of your partner to listen, express his understanding, and offer support. Then switch roles. (If this essentially repeats a conversation you had when preparing to do this exercise, that's okay. Reinforcing support for each other is often helpful.)

Read your lists to each other. One partner reads each item slowly so the other partner has a chance to hear and consider the request. The two of you might want to talk about some items, perhaps reminiscing about when your partner used to do those things or clarifying what is really being asked. Remember that these are requests, not demands. At the end, the listening partner should name one or two items that he is comfortable with and agrees to do.

In the unlikely event that the listener is not comfortable with any items, both of you will benefit from him explaining his discomfort, reaffirming a desire to make you happy, and suggesting other loving actions. Take time to talk through this exchange until you are both comfortable.

Then change roles; the listener becomes the one who shares and vice versa.

Review the exercise after about one week. Share thoughts and feelings about the exercise. In particular, express appreciation for each other's efforts. You might want to repeat the exercise, perhaps making improvements based on feedback, or even add some more ways you can express your love.

♡

On Being Grateful

If you and your partner enjoy each other's company, it seems natural that you would feel good about yourself and develop gratitude for having your partner in your life. Unfortunately, your ability to be grateful in this way might be impaired by attachment struggles. Instead of feeling good about your partner's expressions of love, you might see this as a trait belonging to him, such as him being a loving person, rather than relating to something about you, such as you having an enticing *joie de vivre*. So, instead of feeling better about yourself, you might be grateful to your partner for loving someone so unworthy or flawed as you. To complicate matters, you might build resentments toward your partner, who will inevitably fail at times to meet your needs. Or, even when you do enjoy your current relationship, you might find that it is a painful reminder of relationships in your past that began happily but soured over time. In these and other ways, your positive feelings can transform into unhappiness and reinforce a feeling that you are unworthy of love.

If you relate to this experience, it's very important that you learn to take in your partner's positive view of you and to keep in mind ways in which you value your partner. Review the following two exercises, which are designed to help you do just that. Complete whichever one you think might work for you; or do both if you wish.

Exercise: Mindful Gratitude

You can increase your gratitude by choosing to be aware of and appreciate qualities in yourself and your partner. Consider doing one or more of the following practices on a regular basis:

Focus on what your partner values in you. Work on experiencing acceptance and gratitude for these qualities. Truly listen to her expressions of love and allow them to wash over you as you absorb them.

Focus on what you respect, admire, and are drawn to in your partner. Just think about these things. As positive feelings arise, acknowledge them and choose to be grateful for your partner. When you are upset with your partner for any reason, choose to return to these thoughts as a way to balance (but not dismiss) your negative feelings. This is particularly important to do if you tend to lose sight of your partner's good qualities when you are upset with her.

Focus on the ways in which you and your partner are a great team. Reminisce about good times you've had—whether they were earlier in the day or in years past. Accept, absorb, and treasure all the ways that the two of you create a loving relationship together.

Keep in mind that these practices are likely to show significant and lasting results only if you make doing them an ongoing part of your life.

Exercise: Carry a Gratitude List

The following exercise for nurturing gratitude is based on research conducted by Briñol, Gascó, Petty, and Horcajo (2013). This research found that people can get rid of thoughts, just like they do physical items—by throwing them in the garbage. Similarly, they can keep and treasure thoughts, just like physical items; and in doing so, be more affected by them.

This exercise is structured to help you nurture gratitude in a similar way for positive qualities in your partner and your relationship.

Write about the qualities that you appreciate in your partner. When you complete this, read it over slowly, allowing yourself to really feel good about your partner and to be grateful for having him in your life.

Write about the qualities of your relationship that you appreciate. When you complete this, read it over slowly, allowing yourself to really feel good about your relationship and to be grateful for having it in your life.

Keep the lists close by and accessible. Research indicates that you are more likely to be influenced by this paper if you keep it with you, such as in your pocket. Whether you keep it there or elsewhere, you will benefit from reading it on a regular basis. This will help you to naturally incorporate these thoughts into your attitude toward your partner and your relationship.

It Takes Work to Tango

Just as with dancing, relationships need work and practice. While you must rely on your partner, you must also feel balanced within yourself. Acknowledge that there will be missteps, but focus on the positive. Completing the exercises in this chapter can help you to move in harmony with your inner self and with your partner.

Chapter 10

Working It Out

All truly intimate relationships involve some miscommunication, disagreement, or conflict. However, if you tend to focus with tunnel vision on how you can prevent being rejected and earn your partner's love or attention, you will likely do everything in your power to avoid such issues. You're likely to sweep your own needs and feelings under the rug. This is your way of protecting yourself. In time, though, you'll trip over the ever-growing bump in that rug as you become aware of just how alone you feel in your relationship. You'll experience the hurt that has accumulated and even feel angry with your partner. This is a pattern that cannot ultimately make you happy. Fortunately, there is a better way.

Through compassionate self-awareness, you can learn to value yourself, tolerate your emotions, and be willing to risk vulnerability. You will also be more open to positive feedback from caring people in your life. As a result, you will be better able to the challenge of sharing honestly with your partner, and to truly listening to your partner's experiences without being sidetracked by how they affect you. The result of approaching relationships in this way is that you will be emotionally available for, and capable of, nurturing an intimate connection.

If you continue to be fundamentally open, caring, and expressive when conflict arises, then you are in a perfect position to maintain your strong connection as you work to resolve or manage the conflict. This chapter will guide you through the process of coping with conflict in just such a constructive manner.

Asking for Support

The approach of directly asking for what you want provides you and your partner with the chance to work together on nurturing your relationship. You might find it helpful to focus on two basic practices:

1. Share your feelings, wants, and needs.

2. Ask directly and concretely for what you want from your partner.

Examples:

Heather gets upset when her boyfriend Art goes out with his friends. She generally stews in her feelings but does not share them with Art—which makes her feel more distant from him and worry more about losing him. Finally, she decides to tell him, "When you go out with your friends, I feel abandoned and like I'm not important to you. I want you to have fun with the guys, but this is really hard on me." They talk the problem over and he explains that he enjoys spending time with his buddies, but this is not a replacement for her. After some discussion, they agree that he will always give her enough notice about his plans so she can make plans, too. He even agrees that on nights when she ends up home alone, he will call or text her while he is out or on his way home—just to let her know that he's thinking of her.

Sally frequently goes on business trips, leaving Max to feel lonely and to question how much she really cares for him. He has always been supportive of her career, but he struggles with her traveling so much because he loves spending time with her. He explains this, while also being sure to stress that he truly wants her to follow her dreams. Though they don't come to any solutions for their differing needs, they do feel that they are supportive of each other. They reaffirm their commitment to the relationship and agree to talk and text daily when she's away, which helps.

Of course, not all situations end up working out so well. When your conversations end poorly, be sure to return to them at a time when you are calm. Your goal is to find a way to feel cared about and to really connect with each other on an emotional level, even when you are addressing a difficult issue. The next exercise can help you resolve some of these thorny problems.

Exercise: Starting a Difficult Conversation

The way you bring up an issue to your partner sets the tone of that conversation. In fact, the Gottman Institute, which conducts research related to marriage and relationships, found that not only could they predict the outcome of a fifteen-minute conversation in the first three minutes, they could also predict which couples would divorce and which would remain married (Gottman and Silver, 1999; Carrere and Gottman, 1999). So think carefully about how you start a conversation and follow these guidelines:

Pick an emotionally neutral time to talk. Timing isn't quite everything, but it's a lot. A difficult conversation can only go well if both partners are in a good enough emotional and mental state to deal rationally and calmly with it.

State the problem succinctly. No matter what your partner has done, or what the situation is, the real problem is how it affects you. So state the problem succinctly and get on to the real issue—how you are affected by it.

Do not blame. Going on about all the bad things your partner has done, or directly pointing to faults in his character, will only make him defensive. You won't feel better and he will be more emotionally distant.

Focus on your experience. As much as you might want to lash out at or run from your partner when he's upset you, you mostly want him to understand and care about you. The only way he can do this is if you openly share your thoughts and feelings.

One common method of doing this in a constructive way is to use "I" statements. When you start a sentence with "I," you are telling your partner something about what's going on for you—opening your world to him. By contrast, when you begin a statement with "you," you are probably being critical of your partner and closing down communication.

For instance, imagine saying, "You never do anything romantic anymore." This gets your point across, but you're much more likely to get the response you're looking for by saying, "I wish you'd do something romantic, like how you used to bring me flowers for no reason." Or imagine that you and your partner discussed his tendency to leave his dirty clothes on the floor and he agreed to not do it anymore—but then he did. You might say, "I feel really frustrated with you for doing that. It makes me feel unloved and like I'm your maid. I just feel so alone." Compare that with saying, "You are such a slob and totally insensitive. I don't know why I try to talk to you about anything." Need I say more?

Of course, you can also use "I" statements to be critical, such as, "I think you are an idiot." And "you" statements can be sensitive, such as, "You really have tried to be supportive, but sometimes I'm so upset that I can't take it in." So, when I work with patients, I often have them imagine whom they would be pointing at more when they make the statement; this usually matches the person that they are talking about. The bottom line is that you want to open up about yourself, giving your partner the chance to really "get," support, reassure, and value you.

Be clear about your feelings. You might need to spend some time getting in touch with and identifying your feelings. If you are unable to do this, review the "Identifying Your Emotions" exercise in chapter 6. Once you are clear about your feelings, share them with your partner. For instance, you might say, "I feel sad," or "I feel lonely."

State what your partner can do to meet your needs. Be specific. This often naturally follows from sharing your emotions. For instance, you might say, "I feel unloved, and I need to know that you really love me. So it would be great if you held my hand when we're out together or made plans for us to spend time together." Or you might say, "I feel lonely and want us to be closer. So I'd like it if we could spend more time just sitting and chatting over dinner." If you aren't sure what your partner can do to help you feel better, talk it over together to find a solution.

♡

Talking Through Conflicts

In addition to sharing your feelings and desires, healthy communication requires that you truly listen to and "get" your partner—not just intellectually understand, but see situations through your partner's eyes and empathize with her. To do this, you must be able to put your perspective aside. No cutting off your partner as you give an explanation aimed at making her agree with you. No minimizing or denying your partner's feelings in order to protect yourself from the hurt those feelings elicit. However, as you do this, you do *not* need to agree with your partner or give up on what you want. It's just that you and your partner must take turns listening. It's important that you are both open to sharing, "getting" each other, and talking together supportively and constructively. With this approach, you can promote a sense of safety even in the most personal and vulnerable conversations.

Just as you must be careful about *how* you start a difficult discussion, the power of such a conversation is not just in *what* you talk about, but also *how* you do it. For instance, it helps to be aware that you both have biases and are both fallible. Your willingness to see and admit this can facilitate your openness to feedback, sense of compassion, readiness to apologize, and ability to truly forgive. Overall, for a constructive outcome, you must approach your partner with the intent to really understand him or her, share your experiences, and become emotionally closer. Otherwise, you and your partner will find yourselves living parallel lives, or at odds as you each try to defend your own perspectives.

Below are some guidelines for communicating effectively.

Be a safe haven. I cannot emphasize enough that partners need to feel safe with each other. This can only be nurtured in a conversation by focusing on one partner at a time. If you are addressing an issue, ask your partner to just listen and try to understand what you are saying. Tell him that you want to make sure you've had a chance to get out what's on your mind, and then make sure he gets it before you shift to his thoughts. (This dovetails nicely with the previous exercise, "Starting a Difficult Conversation.")

If your partner is bringing up an issue, really try to understand his perspective. Your goal is to empathize, to try to get as good a sense of what your partner is experiencing as you can. This will naturally help you feel closer to your partner. Also, if your partner senses that you understand and care, he will be less defensive.

A great way to show your partner that you "get" him is to *mirror* what he says. That is, when he's done talking, reflect back in your own words what he is saying, directly or indirectly, about his thoughts and feelings. If you aren't sure that you understand, say so and ask for clarification.

Truly listening without interrupting is often harder than it seems because it's natural to get caught up in your own reactions and want to interject your thoughts. But focus on your partner's distress first. Then, after he feels truly heard, reassured, and valued, you can share your experience—and he'll be more likely to really listen.

Offer positives. It's beneficial to sometimes make note of things you truly appreciate about your partner when discussing a difficult topic. This can prevent you from getting flooded by distressing emotions and negative thoughts about him. Instead, you'll feel at least somewhat grounded by your positive feelings toward your partner. It will also send him the message that you appreciate him, even though you are unhappy with a particular behavior or situation. All of this helps to keep the argument more constructive.

Stay on topic. When arguments get heated, it's easy to jump from topic to topic, or example to example. This can be because you are losing ground and you don't want your partner to win. Or it can be because one negative thought leads to another, and before you know it you are rattling off a list of issues that your partner cannot possibly respond to in a coherent way. But, whatever the reason, no problems are ever resolved when the subject is constantly shifting.

Be respectful. Mutual respect is fundamental to intimate relationships, and there is no good reason to be rude or insulting to your partner. This is true even when you are angry with each other.

If you have a problem with becoming overwhelmed and exploding in anger, take it seriously. This can consume you personally and erode your relationships. Try applying the information about compassionate self-awareness to this issue, finding self-help materials directly related to anger management, or seeking therapy.

The Gift of Forgiveness

Any two people who share their lives and their hearts will at some points hurt each other. It might be out of anger, ignorance, or their own struggles that they can't see past. It might also be caused by a misunderstanding or—sometimes—by caring more about your own happiness than your partner's distress.

Feeling hurt is painful for everyone. But it can be particularly difficult for someone who struggles with attachment-related anxiety. In those cases, it often runs deep, mixing with a sense of being flawed or unworthy of love. Troubling thoughts, feelings, and memories can flood the person. And the resulting self-criticism or hostility toward her or his partner can be powerful and destructive.

If you relate to this, then you need to work on moving past the hurt and learning to forgive. By nurturing forgiveness, you will be giving a gift to *yourself*. It will enable you to let go of anger and bitterness that is burning in *your* heart and soul. You can also consider it a gift to your partner and your relationship. If you believe that your partner generally has your best interests at heart, regrets the harm he's caused you, and will not repeat the offending behavior, forgiveness will allow your relationship to heal. If you do not believe any of that, then it might be time to at least consider moving on. In that case, forgiveness can be your way of wishing your partner well.

Forgiveness doesn't mean saying that an offending behavior is acceptable; rather, it's that you'll leave it in the past. Even so, you might still change your behavior toward your partner because of it. For instance, if your partner is an alcoholic, you might require that he get treatment and refuse to keep alcohol in the house. However, if he gets appropriate help and does his part to remain sober, then you might forgive him by not holding his past against him in the present. This is not something you can just decide in a moment; it involves a process of dealing with feelings within yourself and in your relationship. At a later time (after you've forgiven him), if you believe he has relapsed, you might still air these concerns, but you would do so in a way that focuses on the present. It would certainly make sense to talk about this in the context of the past, but forgiveness means that you wouldn't just dredge up the past without a current reason to do so. I have heard Jack Kornfield, a noted teacher of meditation, express it this way: "Forgiveness is a vow not to carry bitterness into the future… to decide to give up hope for a better past" (2011).

Again, nurturing forgiveness takes time. So have compassion for your struggle and be patient as you work toward healing.

Exercises: Learning to Forgive

What follows is a series of exercises that can help you to move toward forgiveness.

Appreciate being forgiven. Happiness researcher Sonja Lyubomirsky (2008) suggests that people begin the path toward forgiving by appreciating a time when they were forgiven. You might recall a time you were forgiven by a parent, friend, or former partner. Think about why they might have forgiven you and how it felt to be forgiven. Consider how it helped them, you, and your relationship.

Apply understanding and compassion. Keep in mind the upsetting behaviors that you have been unable to forgive as you do the following: Begin by rereading the "Nurturing Awareness of Emotions" section of chapter 6. Then complete the "Identifying Your Emotions" and "Befriending Your Emotions" exercises.

You might also return to the "Mentalizing" section in chapter 6. Keep the hurtful incident in mind as you do. Read it through and complete the exercises "Choose to Be Curious" and "Getting to Know Your Partner from the Inside Out." This will hopefully help you appreciate the situation and your partner's actions from a more understanding perspective.

To be able to forgive, you'll need to practice having compassion for both yourself and your partner. As you go through this process, the goal is to be able to hold on to your own experience while also empathizing with your partner. This can be difficult to do, but it's essential. To help with it, practice going back and forth between the exercises that connect you with your own experience and those that help you to empathize with your partner.

Create a sense of safety. For you to forgive, it's important that you feel emotionally safe. So you need to take reasonable measures to help you feel safe in the present. For instance, if you still want to save your marriage after your spouse has had an affair, you will want to know that she is committed to your relationship and is no longer in contact with the other man. Or if your partner has spent you into the poorhouse, you may want to have control of the money until he gets help and earns back your trust in this area.

Remember that by deciding to forgive, you are not forgetting what happened. You are simply relegating it to the past. As you can see in the above examples, you can still learn from what happened and make decisions based on it. But when you forgive, the difference is that you no longer hold on to the anger, no longer try to make him "pay" for what he did, but instead experience caring and compassion toward your partner.

You will probably have times when you feel pulled to reexperience the past hurt and anger. You will need to talk yourself through them. When thoughts of the offending behavior come to mind, respond with self-compassion. For instance, you might think, "Of course these are difficult memories to leave behind." Then remind yourself that the situation has been addressed, or is being appropriately addressed now. If you can, turn your attention to the present. You might find it helpful to ask your partner for support. It's important that you do this in a nonblaming way. For instance, you might say, "I'm feeling really insecure now. I'm afraid you're going to have another affair and I'll feel like a jerk for ever trusting you again. I need some reassurance from you now." (The previous exercises in how to start and talk through difficult conversations can help you with this.)

Finally, with reassurance that you are emotionally safe, focus on the positives in your relationship and on the love he expresses to you now. Depending on your particular circumstance, you might need more guidance and support in this area. If so, search out self-help materials or individual or couples therapy.

Moving On

There may come a time when you seriously question whether your relationship is right for you, and you ask yourself whether you should stick with it or end it. To decide this, you need to take a good, hard look at your relationship. You might find that you know what you "have" to do, and that the real problem is doing it. Or your challenge might be making a decision even when you aren't so sure. Neither situation is easy, but the next exercises will provide some guidance.

Exercise: Is It Worth It?

If you are torn about whether to end your relationship, then you need to assess how healthy the relationship is for you, as well as your desire to stay in the relationship, your willingness to work on it, and whether you think your partner has an interest in—and the ability to—meet your needs. To guide you through this, think about the following:

Consider how well your relationship fits the criteria for a healthy relationship. You may remember that you are likely to feel happiest in a relationship if your partner can do the following for you:

Be emotionally available:

- Be responsive to your wants and needs.

- Value you as a person, not just for what you can do for him.

Be a safe haven:

- Be supportive and reassuring, especially during difficult times.

- Comfort you when you are upset.

Be a secure base:

- Encourage and support you in pursuing your interests.

To feel like an equal, you will also want to be there for your partner in these same ways. This, of course, means that your partner must be open to sharing his wants and needs with you, turning to you in times of distress, and looking to you for support in pursuing his interests. Your relationship does not need to be perfectly balanced in each of these areas, but you do need to be comfortable with the balance that exists.

Acknowledge your emotional needs and desires. Look back at the exercises in chapter 8 in which you imagined your perfect partner and perfect relationship. Not that anyone or any relationship is perfect, but how are your current partner and relationship measuring up?

Express your needs directly. While you want a partner who generally tries to meet your wants and needs, you are responsible for letting those be known. Have you been clear about this? For instance, you might sometimes ask for reassurance that he loves you or say that you want to spend more time together. If you have not communicated clearly and directly about what you want, then you need to think about why this is the case, and perhaps return to the exercises earlier in this chapter on communicating effectively with your partner.

Consider whether your partner has consistently treated you with respect. A partner who really wants you to be happy will consistently give you the message that you are a priority and worthy of his efforts to try to please you. As you think about whether this characterizes your partner, you might find it helpful to talk with someone other than your partner—someone else whom you trust and respect. If you realize that your partner has frequently made it evident that you are not a priority and has disrespected you as someone who "has issues"—that you are too needy, for instance, or too insecure—then you are dealing with someone who is not acting as an engaged, supportive, and caring partner. It is time to move on. Conversely, if you have not treated your partner with respect, then it is time for you to reconsider your own actions. By trying to live up to the standard of always being respectful—even when you are upset—you are doing your part in nurturing a healthy and respectful relationship.

Compare the picture of your relationship with your experience. Just because your partner looks to the world like the perfect catch, this does not mean that he is. Some people treat their partners better in public than they do in private. And sometimes, even when someone looks like a good match "on paper," there might be something about who that person is that makes him or her a bad fit. If you think either of these situations describes your relationship, talk with a caring friend who can validate your experience and reinforce that your feelings matter. If your friend challenges you with the suggestion that your insecurity is affecting your perceptions and is the real issue, then give some serious thought to this. Talk it through with this or another friend and decide for yourself whether you would be better off working on your relationship or ending it.

Exercise: Letting Go

If you decide to leave your partner, it's important to formulate a plan that will help you to walk away and keep on walking. So consider these recommendations:

Build a support system ahead of time. As Levine and Heller (2010) point out, breakups are painful and you will do best if you have supportive people to lean on. This means being honest with them about your struggles so that they can understand your circumstance and truly support your decision to end your relationship.

One of the most difficult parts of leaving a relationship is that your partner was the one you relied on (or had a fantasy of relying on) for connection, support, caring, and reassurance. Your partner may be the one person you looked to for a sense of mattering in this world. By having a support system in place, you can turn to these other people to serve as both a safe haven, to comfort you when you're distressed, and a secure base, encouraging you to pursue your own interests. While feeling like an important part of other people's lives doesn't replace having a partner, it can give you a sense of belonging and can make all the difference in how you feel about yourself.

Let yourself mourn. This is a natural response when you lose an important person in your life—even if you are better off without him. Friends might tell you, "He's not worth it," but the fact is that no longer having him in your life is still a loss. So feel the sadness, anger, hurt, or whatever else you feel. But keep putting one foot in front of the other as you walk away. With time, he will be far behind and you will stop looking over your shoulder as your new life becomes more engaging.

Remind yourself of your value and strengths. This can be particularly difficult to do when you are down. Consider what family and friends appreciate about you. If you are inclined to dismiss or minimize this, don't be so hasty. These people choose to interact with you because they want to—even family members don't *have to* stay in contact. You might also find it helpful to refer back to the chapter 7 exercises, *Discover the Value in You* and *Be Your Own Best Friend*.

Choose healthy ways of coping. While it is always a good idea to take care of yourself, this is especially important when you are going though a difficult time. Unfortunately, this is also when you are more likely to give in to impulses to seek immediate gratification, such as with food, alcohol, sex, or shopping—or to just withdraw from the world. It's okay to respond in these ways sometimes, but you still need to be smart about it. You'll only make matters worse by eating your way up a size or more, or buying a Porsche on a Hyundai budget. And hiding out at home never made anyone happy in the long term. So make the effort to engage in the things you know will eventually help you feel better: eat healthily, exercise regularly, get enough sleep, socialize, and return to spiritual practices if you have them, as well as to other activities you normally enjoy.

Engage in meaningful work. When people feel that they are doing something that is personally meaningful, they are more likely to become truly engaged in it. And a sense of engagement is a wonderful antidote to feeling disconnected. Examples of such work are volunteering at a school or homeless shelter, gardening, going back to school for an advanced degree, or writing a book (yes, that's my personal example). You can, of course, choose more than one activity to fold into your life.

While your choices do not have to include doing something for and with other people, helping others—and doing it through direct contact—can provide an additional sense of connection and of having value. It is also linked to the helpers' feeling happier.

Refocus on the moment. If you get lost in your painful feelings, try refocusing on whatever you are doing in the present moment. For help with this, refer back to the steps in the chapter 7 exercise "Embodying Your Body."

Be prepared for the urge to reunite. There is a good chance that you will, at some point, entertain the idea of going back to your partner. You might remember all the good times or think that maybe you can do it differently this time. Before picking up the phone or "happening" to run into him, think seriously about your situation. Acknowledge how difficult it is to stay away, but also think about how hard it was to be in the relationship. If you are flooded with positive memories, do a reality check. Did those enjoyable times really characterize your relationship? Or were there more painful times that outweighed them?

Ask yourself why you decided to leave. If you know why, but have trouble keeping those things strongly in mind, write a list (during one of your stronger moments) that you can refer back to. Also, before reaching out to your former partner, reach out to a supportive friend to talk over the situation. Finally, assuming that you know your decision to leave was the right one, remind yourself in weak moments that "this, too, shall pass."

Be forgiving of yourself if you go back. Even if you make the above efforts, you might find yourself texting your old boyfriend with the secret hope of reuniting, or find yourself back in his arms before you fully realize what you've done. As soon as you realize your mistake, put an end to it. Remember, everyone has weak moments; so forgive yourself. If you need help nurturing self-compassion, the "Be Your Own Best Friend" exercise in chapter 7 might help. The sooner you can put your mistake in perspective, the better off you'll be.

Breakups are never easy, but armed with an understanding of what went wrong (not only this time, but also so many times in the past), you now have a better chance for a healthier, more secure relationship.

♡

Closing Thoughts

Hopefully, through reading and applying the information in this book, you have a new appreciation for your difficulties in romantic relationships. You can see that they are expressions of struggles with how you relate to yourself, as well as to your partner. You can also identify the path toward a happy, healthy romantic relationship, and have made significant progress down that path. Part of the beauty of enjoying a secure relationship with a partner is that it also encourages and reinforces a secure sense of yourself.

If you do the work laid out in this book, you *will* become happier—in your romantic relationship, in your other relationships, within yourself, and in your life. There's no doubt that this takes focus, persistence, and effort. But the benefits are tremendous!

Seeking Professional Help

By finishing this book, you've taken great strides, but it still might not be enough. For instance, if your partner is not doing her part despite seeming to want to be together, or you seem to be unable to break free of your patterns of anxious attachment, then seriously consider couples therapy. Or if your attachment-related anxiety overwhelms your efforts to develop a sense of self-acceptance or your ability to feel safe in relationships, consider individual therapy.

You can apply insights from this book to therapy; and you can even help your therapy along by sharing them in sessions so that the therapist can integrate them into the treatment process. John Bowlby (1989), the man who first proposed the idea of an attachment system, explained that therapy can help people develop more secure styles of relating to others (Mikulincer and Shaver, 2007).

It is essential for you to develop a sense of your therapist as a safe haven and a secure base. With this foundation, you will feel supported in pursuing personal interests and opportunities for growth, and you will also feel safe enough to explore your insecurities. Your therapist can guide you in gaining greater awareness of painful feelings, negative self-perceptions, and problematic behaviors. You'll learn to consciously recognize your own well-intentioned but misguided efforts to develop a sense of safety and reassurance in your relationships.

Although you certainly want to find an experienced and capable therapist, it's essential that you also find a professional with whom you have a good rapport. Because therapy involves heartfelt discussions that will leave you feeling vulnerable, you need to feel as emotionally safe as possible with your therapist.

In many ways, the work you do in therapy naturally develops your ability for compassionate self-awareness. Moreover, by understanding compassionate self-awareness, you can talk more directly about it. This discussion can facilitate the work of therapy, helping you to effectively change your self-perceptions and your ways of relating to others.

You Can Do This

Your relationship problems can feel overwhelming, but when they do, remember that there *is* a path to happier, healthier connections. You can find a life partner who is there to support, encourage, and love you, just as you can be there to support, encourage, and love him. The way to do this is what this book has been all about. It offers you a way to focus compassionately on your experiences in the moment, enabling you to nurture yourself and your relationship (or your potential relationship). Together, these actions *will* free your love from insecurity!

References

I am tremendously grateful for the work of the many researchers and theorists who have been so influential in this book. My thoughts with regards to attachment theory and compassionate self-awareness have been possible only with the foundation that they laid. Though you will find a substantial number of them among these references, I want to express special gratitude to a few. With regards to attachment theory, I am particularly indebted to John Bowlby, Mary Ainsworth, Mary Main, Karen Bartholomew, Peter Fonagy, Phillip Shaver, Jude Cassidy, Mario Mikulincer, Chris Fraley, and David Wallin. It was also helpful to read the work of others, such as Sue Johnson, Amir Levine, and Rachel Heller, who have shared ideas about attachment theory with the general public. William Swann has provided compelling ideas with his theory about and research on self-verification. With regards to my ideas about compassionate self-awareness, I am particularly indebted to Kristin Neff, Christopher Germer, Jon Kabat-Zinn, the many researchers of mindfulness and meditation, and Buddhism. Many of these ideas only resonate with the general population because of those who have successfully shared them with the community at large, such as Jon Kabat-Zinn and Jack Kornfield.

Ainsworth, M. R. S., M. C. Blehar, E. Waters, and S. Wall. 1978. *Patterns of Attachment: Assessed in the Strange Situation and At Home.* Hillsdale, NJ: Erlbaum.

Baera, R., E. Lykins, and J. Peters. 2012. "Mindfulness and Self-Compassion as Predictors of Psychological Wellbeing in Long-Term Meditators and Matched Nonmeditators." *Journal of Positive Psychology* 7: 230–238.

Barnard, L., and J. Curry. 2011. "Self-Compassion: Conceptualizations, Correlates, and Interventions." *Review of General Psychology* 15: 289–303.

Bartholomew, K., and L. Horowitz. 1991. "Attachment Styles Among Young Adults: A Test of a Four-Category Model." *Journal of Personality and Social Psychology* 61: 226–244.

Bollas, C. 1987. *The Shadow of the Object: Psychoanalysis of the Unthought Known*. New York: Columbia University Press.

Bowlby, J. 1961. "Childhood Mourning and Its Implications for Psychiatry." In *The Making and Breaking of Affectional Bonds* by J. Bowlby. New York: Routledge.

Bowlby, J. 1989. *The Making and Breaking of Affectional Bonds*. New York: Routledge.

Brennan, K., C. L. Clark, and P. R. Shaver. 1998. "Self-Report Measurement of Adult Romantic Attachment: An Integrative Overview." In *Attachment Theory and Close Relationships*, edited by J. A. Simpson and W. S. Rholes. New York: Guilford Press.

Briñol, P., M. Gascó, R. Petty, and J. Horcajo. 2013. "Treating Thoughts as Material Objects Can Increase or Decrease Their Impact on Evaluation." *Psychological Science* 24: 41–47.

Burton, R. 2008. *On Being Certain: Believing You Are Right Even When You're Not*. New York: St. Martin's Press.

Carrere, S., and J. Gottman. 1999. "Predicting Divorce Among Newlyweds from the First Three Minutes of a Marital Conflict Discussion." *Family Process* 38: 293–301.

Collins, N. L. 1996. "Working Models of Attachment: Implications for Explanation, Emotions, and Behavior." *Journal of Personality and Social Psychology* 71: 810–32.

Davis, D., and J. Hayes. 2012. "What Are the Benefits of Mindfulness?" *Monitor on Psychology* 43: 64–70.

Drigotas, S., C. Rusbult, J. Wieselquist, and S. Whitton. 1999. "Close Partner as Sculptor of the Ideal Self: Behavioral Affirmation and the Michelangelo Phenomenon." *Journal of Personality and Social Psychology* 77: 293–323.

Feeney, J. a. 2008. "Adult Romantic Attachment: Developments in the Study of Couple Relationships." In *Handbook of Attachment: Theory, Research, and Clinical Applications*, edited by J. Cassidy and P. Shaver. New York: Guilford Press.

Feeney, J. A., P. Noller, and M. Hanrahan. 1994. "Assessing Adult Attachment." In *Attachment in Adults: A Clinical and Developmental Perspective*, edited by M. B. Sperling and W. H. Berman. New York: Guilford Press.

Fonagy, P., G. Gergely, E. Jurist, and M. Target. 2002. *Affect Regulation, Mentalization, and the Development of the Self*. New York: Other Press.

Fraley, C., A. Vicary, C. Brumbaugh, and G. Roisman. 2011. "Patterns of Stability in Adult Attachment: An Empirical Test of Two Models of Continuity and Change." *Journal of Personality and Social Psychology* 101: 974–992.

Fredrickson, B. 2001. "The Role of Positive Emotions in Positive Psychology: The Broaden-and-Build Theory of Positive Emotions." *American Psychologist* 56: 218–226.

Germer, C. 2009. *The Mindful Path to Self-Compassion: Freeing Yourself from Destructive Thoughts and Emotions*. New York: Guilford Press.

Goldman, B., and M. Kernis. 2002. "The Role of Authenticity in Healthy Psychological Functioning and Subjective Well-Being." *Annals of the American Psychotherapy Association* 5: 18–20.

Gottman, J. 2002. *Marital Therapy: A Research-Based Approach: The Two-Day Workshop for Clinicians* (Compact disc.) Seattle: Gottman Institute.

Gottman, J., and N. Silver. 1999. *The Seven Principles for Making Marriage Work: A Practical Guide from the Country's Foremost Relationship Expert*. New York: Three Rivers Press.

Griffin, D. W., and K. Bartholomew. 1994. "The Metaphysics of Measurement: The Case of Adult Attachment." In *Advances in*

Personal Relationships (Vol. 5, *Attachment Processes in Adulthood*), edited by K. Bartholomew and D. Perlman. London: Jessica Kingsley Publishers.Hazan, C., and P. Shaver. 1987. "Romantic Love Conceptualized as an Attachment Process." *Journal of Personality and Social Psychology* 52: 511–524.

Hutcherson, C., E. Seppala, and J. Gross. 2008. "Loving-Kindness Meditation Increases Social Connectedness." *Emotion* 8: 720–724.

Johnson, S. 2008. *Hold Me Tight: Seven Conversations for a Lifetime of Love*. New York: Little, Brown and Company.

Kabat-Zinn, J. 1994. *Wherever You Go, There You Are*. New York: Hyperion.

Kornfield, J. (2011, April). *The Wise Heart and the Mindful Brain*. Talk presented at the Skirball Center for the Performing Arts, New York University, New York.

Levine, A., and R. Heller. 2010. *Attached: The New Science of Adult Attachment and How It Can Help You Find—and Keep—Love*. New York: Penguin.

Lyubomirsky, S. 2008. *The How of Happiness: A Scientific Approach to Getting the Life You Want*. New York: Penguin Press.

Lyubomirsky, S., and L. Ross. 1997. "Hedonic Consequences of Social Comparison: A Contrast of Happy and Unhappy People." *Journal of Personality and Social Psychology* 73: 1141–1157.

Mikulincer, M., and P. Shaver. 2007. *Attachment in Adulthood: Structure, Dynamics, and Change*. New York: Guilford Press.

Mikulincer, M., and P. Shaver. 2008. "Adult Attachment and Affect Regulation." In *Handbook of Attachment: Theory, Research, and Clinical Applications*, edited by J. Cassidy and P. Shaver. New York: Guilford Press.

Neff, K. 2008. "Self-Compassion: Moving Beyond the Pitfalls of a Separate Self-Concept." In *Transcending Self-Interest: Psychological Explorations of the Quiet Ego*, edited by J. Bauer and H. Wayment. Washington, DC: APA Books.

Neff, K., S. Rude, and K. Kirkpatrick. 2007. "An Examination of Self-Compassion in Relation to Positive Psychological Functioning and Personality Traits." *Journal of Research in Personality* 41: 908–916.

Pines, A. 2005. *Falling in Love*. New York: Routledge.

Shaver, P., and C. Hazan. 1988. "A Biased Overview of the Study of Love." *Journal of Social and Personal Relationships* 5: 473–501.

Simpson, J. A., S. W. Rholes, and D. Phillips. 1996. "Conflict in Close Relationships: An Attachment Perspective." *Journal of Personality and Social Psychology* 71: 899–914.

Slade, A. 2008. "The Implications of Attachment Theory and Research for Adult Psychotherapy: Research and Clinical Perspectives." In *Handbook of Attachment: Theory, Research, and Clinical Applications*, edited by J. Cassidy and P. Shaver. New York: Guilford Press.

Swann, W., P. Rentfrow, and J. Guinn. 2003. "Self-Verification: The Search for Coherence." In *Handbook of Self and Identity*, edited by M. Leary and J. Tangney. New York: Guilford Press.

Swann, W.B., Jr., A. Stein-Seroussi, and R. B. Giesler. 1992. "Why People Self-Verify." *Journal of Personality and Social Psychology* 62: 392–401.

Tavris, C., and E. Aronson. 2007. "Self-Justification in Public and Private Spheres: What Cognitive Dissonance Theory Teaches Us About Cheating, Justice, Memory, Psychotherapy, Science, and the Rest of Life." *General Psychologist* 42: 4–7.

Tavris, C., and E. Aronson. 2007. *Mistakes Were Made (But Not by Me): Why We Justify Foolish Beliefs, Bad Decisions, and Hurtful Acts*. New York: Harcourt.

Wallin, D. 2007. *Attachment in Psychotherapy*. New York: Guilford Press.

Winnicott, D. W. 1953. "Transitional Objects and Transitional Phenomena: A Study of the First Not-Me Possession." *International Journal of Psychoanalysis* 34: 89–97.

Leslie Becker-Phelps, PhD, is a licensed psychologist, author, and speaker. She writes *The Art of Relationships* blog for WebMD and is the relationship expert for WebMD's relationships and coping community. She also writes the blog *Making Change* for *Psychology Today*. Becker-Phelps previously served at Somerset Medical Center in Somerville, NJ, as director of women's psychological services and chief of psychology in the department of psychiatry. She lives with her husband and two sons in Basking Ridge, NJ. Find out more about her at www.drbecker-phelps.com.